HOW TO IMPROVE YOUR CHARISMA?

Secrets To Stop Anxiety With Charismatic Communication Guaranteed Charm & Social Skills Improvement + Small Talk Guide

---

TABLE OF CONTENTS

INTRODUCTION

Charisma has always been a fascinating and contentious topic. Have you ever fantasized about being as charismatic as Bill Clinton or as intriguing as Steve Jobs? If you already have some charisma and want to improve it, or you've been wishing for a little of the magic but don't think you're the charismatic kind, I have good news for you: charisma is an ability that can be learned and practised.

What Would Charisma Help You with?

Consider how different your life would be if you knew that the moment you walked into a room, people would notice you, want to hear what you have to say and be willing to gain your approval.

This is a way of life for charismatic people. Their presence has an impact on others. People are attracted to them magnetically and feel compelled to assist them in whatever way they can. Charismatic people seem to live enchanted lives: they seem to have it all. People who are charismatic seem to have a charmed life: they have more romantic opportunities, make more money, and are less stressed.

People would like you, trust you, and want to follow you if you have charisma. It can influence whether you're seen as a follower or a leader, whether your ideas are accepted, and how well your projects are executed. Whether you like it or not, the charm has the power to make people want to do what you want.

In the market, charisma is, of course, crucial. It will assist you in achieving your target, whether you are looking for a new job or want to progress within your current company. According to several reports, charismatic individuals have higher success scores and are seen as more successful by their supervisors and subordinates.

If you want to be a leader, charisma is essential. It gives you a leg up on the competition when it comes to recruiting and retaining top talent. People want to partner with you, your team, and your organization because of it. According to research, those who follow charismatic leaders perform better, have a more meaningful work experience, and have more faith in their leaders than those who follow successful yet non-charismatic leaders.

Charisma is what allows a good salesperson to sell five times as much as his peers in the same field. It's the difference amongst entrepreneurs who have investors knocking on their doors and others who must beg a bank for a loan.

Outside of the corporate world, the influence of charisma is equally important. It's helpful for stay-at-home moms who need to influence their children, teachers, or other members of the group. It can be a valuable resource for high school students preparing for college interviews or running for positions of leadership in student organizations. It can assist people in becoming more successful with their peers and becoming more comfortable in social situations. Patients prefer charismatic doctors, who are in higher demand, and their patients are more likely to follow through with the medical procedures they recommend. When things go wrong, they're much less likely to be sued. Even in science and academia, charismatic people are more likely to be published, to receive research funding from industry grants, and to teach the most sought-after courses. After lectures, the professor, who is often surrounded by admiring students, has charisma.

It Isn't Magic; It's a Collection of Learned Behaviors

People are not born charismatic—innately magnetic from birth, contrary to common opinion. If charisma were a natural trait, charismatic people would still be enthralling, but this isn't the case.

Charisma can be present one moment and missing the next, except for the most entertaining superstar.

Charisma is the product of particular nonverbal actions, not an innate or magical personal attribute, as comprehensive research has shown in recent years. Here is one of the reasons why charisma levels fluctuate: whether or not anyone exhibits certain habits determines whether or not they have charisma.

Have you ever had the sensation of being fully in control of a situation? A time when you appeared to impress others—even if it was just for a brief moment—and the people around you said, "Wow!" Since we believe charismatic people are irresistible at all times, we don't actually think of these encounters as charisma or consider ourselves charismatic. They're not.

One of the reasons charisma is misunderstood as inherent is that, like all other social skills, charismatic habits are acquired early on. In reality, most people aren't even aware that they're learning them. They're simply experimenting with different habits, observing the effects, and fine-tuning them. The actions eventually become instinctive.

Numerous well-known charismatic personalities worked hard to develop their charisma, gradually increasing it. But, since we just see them at their most charismatic, it's difficult to believe they weren't always so impressive.

Steve Jobs, the former CEO of Apple and widely regarded as one of the most charismatic CEOs of the decade, did not start out that way. In reality, if you watch his early talks, you'll notice that he came across as shy and awkward, ranging from overly dramatic to nerdy. Jobs' charisma grew over time, and his public appearances reflect this.

Sociologists, psychologists, and cognitive and behavioural scientists have also studied charisma. Clinical laboratory studies, cross-sectional and longitudinal survey testing, and qualitative interpretative analysis have all been used to investigate it. Presidents, students of all ages, military leaders, and company executives ranging from low-level administrators to CEOs have all been the subjects of these studies. We now recognize charisma as a collection of behaviours as a result of such a study.

How Does Charismatic Behaviour Appear?

When we encounter anyone for the first time, we immediately decide whether they are a possible friend or foe, as well as whether they have the ability to carry out their intentions. We're trying to figure out who has the most power and who has the best intentions. "Would you be willing to lift mountains for me?" And would you be interested in doing so?" We try to determine how much control he or she has in order to answer the first question. We try to figure out how much he or she likes us in order to answer the second question. When you meet a charismatic person, you get the feeling that they are powerful and that they really care for you.

The formula for charisma is actually very straightforward.

All you have to do is offer the appearance of having both a lot of power and a lot of warmth since charismatic behaviours combine these two qualities. The power question is, "Do you want to fight or flee?" The warm question is, "Friend or foe?"

Both of these characteristics have a final dimension: there is a presence. People often discuss the individual's exceptional "presence" when describing their experience of seeing charisma in motion, whether they encountered people with great charisma or not.

The most requested element of charisma is presence; it turns out that presence is the true core component of charisma, the cornerstone upon which all else is constructed. When you're with a charismatic master, you not only sense his strength and a warm sense of engagement, but you also sense that he's fully present with you right now.

Charisma has been studied and turned into a science. You'll learn charisma in a systematic, methodical manner, with practical lessons that you can apply right away in the real world. And, unlike the people who learned by trial and error, you won't have to spend any time finding out what works and what doesn't. You can jump right to the tried-and-true methods for increasing charisma.

It takes effort to become more charismatic—work that can be difficult, uncomfortable, and even frightening at times. It is, however, extremely satisfying, both in terms of how you relate to yourself and how others relate to you. It entails maintaining your mental ecosystem, respecting and attending to your own needs, as well as recognizing and projecting the habits that cause others to perceive you as charismatic.

This book will assist you in this endeavour. It will equip you with practical tools for projecting the three key characteristics of charisma: presence, strength, and warmth. You'll feel a stronger sense of personal magnetism when you use them, and if it were already powerful, you'd have more influence over the charismatic force. You'll learn how to control it and wield it with finesse. In any case, you'll also learn how to pick the right kind of charisma for your personality and goals.

You'll have an inside look at what goes on in charismatic people's heads—and bodies.

Practical magic is what you'll find here: unique insight derived from a range of sciences that reveals what charisma is and how it works. You'll learn both the perspectives and the tools you'll need to put your newfound experience to work. Every time you meet someone, the universe will become your laboratory, and you will have the opportunity to experiment.

You'll be able to learn how to be charismatic even in stressful circumstances once you've learned the fundamentals, such as when you're having a career-changing interview, interacting with a difficult person, or giving a presentation. You'll learn the insider secrets to living life as a charismatic person until you know how to access charisma at will.

You'll discover how to become more convincing, powerful, and motivating. You'll learn how to exude charisma, which is described as the ability to move around a room and make people say, "Wow, who's that?"

CHAPTER ONE

CHARISMA UNRAVELED

If they realize it or not, charismatic people choose actions that make others feel a certain way. Anyone will pick up on these habits and perfect them. In reality, researchers were able to lift and lower people's charisma levels as if they were turning dial-in controlled laboratory experiments.

Contrary to popular belief, you do not need to be inherently outgoing, physically beautiful, or alter your attitude to be charismatic. You will dramatically increase your personal charisma and reap the benefits both in business and in everyday life, regardless of where you start.

The most prevalent charisma fallacy is that to be charismatic, you must be automatically boisterous or outgoing. One of the most intriguing research findings is that an introvert may be extremely charismatic. Introverts can feel deficient and uncool in Western society because we put too much focus on extroverts' skills and abilities. Introversion, on the other hand, is not a fatal flaw. Indeed, as we'll see, it can be a significant benefit for certain types of charisma.

It's also a fallacy that being charismatic requires being beautiful. Countless charismatic personalities fell well short of traditional beauty expectations.

Yes, good looks will help you get ahead. However, even if you don't have a striking face or figure, you can still be charismatic. In reality, charisma will increase your attractiveness. In randomized trials, participants' levels of attractiveness were substantially higher when they were told to demonstrate particular charismatic behaviours.

Finally, you would not be required to alter your personality. You don't have to push yourself into one personality type or do anything that goes against your nature to become more charismatic.

Rather, you will acquire new skills.

You'll learn how to adopt a charismatic pose, warm up your eye contact, and modulate your voice in ways that compel people to pay attention during charisma training. Three fast tips to improve your charm in a conversation:

• At the end of each sentence, lower your voice intonation.

• Reduce the number of times you nod and how easily you nod.

• Take a two-second pause before speaking.

As you can see, these are minor adjustments rather than significant value changes. Your personality will remain unchanged for as long as you want.

Would these new abilities and actions come across as strange at first? It's possible. But, when you first learned how to brush your teeth, it felt the same way, even though it's now (hopefully) a routine you do every day without thinking about it. Like all new skills, charismatic behaviours can feel uncomfortable at first, but with practice, much like walking, talking, or driving, they will become second nature. This book will walk you through the process of learning these habits and making them your own.

We recognize that mastering chess, singing, or hitting a fastball takes deliberate practice. Charisma is an ability that can be learned by deliberate practice, and we get to use our charisma tools on a regular basis because we work with people all the time.

Since I've helped countless clients improve their charisma by deliberate practice, I know it can be improved.

You will improve your charisma if you follow the directions in this book. And once these habits become second nature, they continue to work in the background without you having to think about them—and you'll continue to reap the benefits as a result.

HOW WOULD THIS BENEFIT YOU?

Reverse-engineered the science of charisma by studying the behavioural and cognitive science that underpins it and extracting the most useful methods and techniques. This book will assist you in putting the science into motion so that you can learn faster.

PROVIDING YOU WITH THE RESOURCES THAT WILL YIELD THE BEST RESULTS

Offering you the latest, most powerful methods from a wide variety of disciplines—from behavioural, cognitive, and neuroscience to meditation; from peak-performance athletic training to Hollywood Method acting—as well as the resources that will give you the best return on your investment.

You'll get the science when it's important (or entertaining, or fascinating), and you'll get the practical tools, too. This book will teach you strategies that you can use right away to develop the skills and self-confidence you need to perform at your best.

However, simply reading this book will not provide you with all of its advantages. You'd be doing yourself a disservice if you skipped any of the exercises, no matter how strange or even unpleasant they might be at times. To be good, you must be willing to put in the effort to put what you've learned into practice. When an exercise instructs you to close your eyes and envisions a scenario, do so fully. Get a sheet of paper and a writing pen if you're asked to type out a scenario.

There's no way around doing the exercises. Skimming through them with the sincere intention of finishing them "someday" is insufficient, as is focusing only on the exercises that seem simple or interesting. If you're asked to do something, it's for a reason, and it'll have a significant effect on your charisma.

Any of the strategies you'll learn here will yield immediate results, such as how to be charismatic while speaking to small or large audiences. Others can take weeks to complete. Some of them can come as a surprise, such as how your toes will help you maximize your charisma.

CHAPTER TWO

THE CHARISMATIC BEHAVIORS: PRESENCE, POWER, AND WARMTH

The three core elements of charismatic behaviour are presence, power, and warmth. These elements are influenced by both our conscious actions and uncontrollable factors. People pick up on messages we send through small changes in our body language that we don't even realize we're sending. We'll look at how these signals can be influenced in this chapter. We must choose mental states that allow our body language, words, and behaviours to flow together and express the three core elements of charisma in order to be charismatic. We'll start there because presence is the foundation for everything else.

A SENSE OF BEING PRESENT

Have you ever felt as if only half of your mind was present during a conversation while the other half was preoccupied with something else? Do you believe the other person was aware of your presence?

If you're not fully engaged in a conversation, your eyes may glaze over, or your facial reactions may be delayed by a fraction of a second. Because the human mind can read facial expressions in as little as seventeen milliseconds, even the tiniest delays in your reactions will be noticed by the person you're speaking with.

We may believe that we can create a false sense of presence. We may believe that we can act as if we are listening. We believe that as long as we appear attentive, it's fine to let our minds wander. However, we are mistaken. People can tell when we aren't fully engaged in a conversation. Our body language sends a message that other people, at least subconsciously, read and react to.

You've probably had the experience of conversing with someone who wasn't paying attention. Perhaps they appeared to be "going through the motions" of listening to you in order to avoid offending you. They didn't appear to be paying full attention in any way.

What were your feelings at the time? Have you been brushed off? Are you annoyed? Is it just bad?

Not only can a lack of presence be visible, but it can also be perceived as inauthentic, leading to even more negative emotional outcomes. It's nearly impossible to build trust, rapport, or loyalty when you're perceived as dishonest. It's also impossible to have charisma.

Presence is a skill that can be learned. You can improve it with practice and patience, just like any other skill (from painting to playing the piano). Being present simply means being aware of what is going on in the present moment. It entails being aware of what is going on rather than being preoccupied with your own thoughts.

Now that you understand the cost of a lack of presence try the exercise on the next page to put yourself to the test, see how present you are and learn three simple techniques to boost your charisma in personal interactions right away.

Adapted from mindfulness disciplines, here are a few techniques for staying present. All you need is a relatively quiet location where you can close your eyes for one minute (whether standing or sitting) and a way to keep track of time.

One minute has been set on the timer. Close your eyes and concentrate on one of three things: the sounds surrounding you, your breathing, or the sensations in your toes.

1. Sounds: Listen to what's going on around you. "Imagine your ears are satellite dishes, passively and objectively registering sounds," a meditation teacher advised.

2. Concentrate on your breath and the sensations it causes in your nostrils or stomach as it enters and exits. Concentrate on one breath at a time, attempting to notice everything about it. Consider your breath to be someone to whom you want to devote your undivided attention.

3. The sensations in your toes: Pay attention to the sensations in your toes. This forces your mind to go through your body, allowing you to immerse yourself in the present moment's physical sensations.

So, how did it turn out? So, how did that go? Did you find your mind on a regular basis? Even when you tried your hardest to stay present, did your mind constantly wander? Staying fully present isn't always easy, as you've noticed. This is due to two main factors.

To begin with, our brains are wired to pay attention to novel stimuli, such as sights, smells, and sounds. We're hardwired to be distracted, to be drawn in by any new stimulus: It could be crucial! It might eat us! This trait was crucial to our forefathers' survival. Imagine two tribe members scouring the plains for signs of the antelope that will feed their family. In the distance, something flickers. Who was the tribesman whose interest wasn't immediately piqued? He isn't one of our forefathers.

The second reason is that our culture encourages people to be distracted. Our natural tendencies are exacerbated by the constant influx of stimulation we receive. This can eventually lead to a state of continuous partial attention, in which we never give anything our complete attention. We're always partially oblivious to what's going on around us.

So don't be too hard on yourself if you find it difficult to be fully present on a regular basis. This is completely natural. For almost all of us, being present is difficult. Even the most accomplished meditators can have their minds wander during their practice. In fact, during intensive meditation retreats, this is a common source of jokes (yes, there are such things as meditation jokes).

The good news is that even a small increase in your present capacity can have a significant impact on those around you. Since so few of us are ever completely present, even a few moments of full presence can have a big effect.

TRY TO DO THIS THE NEXT TIME YOU'RE IN A CONVERSATION

Try and check if your mind is fully engaged or if it is wandering elsewhere the next time you're in a conversation (including preparing your next sentence). Focus on your breath or toes for a second to get yourself back to the present moment, then return your attention to the other individual.

Don't get discouraged if you didn't completely succeed in the one-minute exercise. Simply by practising presence, you were able to boost your charisma right then and there. You're still ahead of the trend because you've acquired the paradigm change (awareness of the value of presence and the expense of not having it). It will be well worth your time to stop reading right now and not continue.

Here's how this could play out in a real-life situation for you. Let's say a coworker comes into your office and asks for your opinion on something. You only have a few minutes before your next meeting, and you're worried that this will take longer than you anticipated.

If you let your mind wander as he speaks to you, you'll not only feel nervous and have trouble focusing, but you'll also seem restless and distracted. Your coworker may conclude that you don't care enough about him or his problem to pay attention to him.

Instead, remember to use one of the fast remedies, such as concentrating for a second on your breath or toes, and you will be brought back to the present moment immediately. This full presence will be visible in your eyes and face, and the person speaking to you will notice it by only giving them a few by the person who is conversing with you. They will feel respected and listened to if you give them just a few moments of your full attention. When you're present, it displays in your body language, which boosts your charisma.

Being charismatic is determined by how fully present you are in each interaction, not by how much time you have. You will stand out from the crowd if you have the ability to be fully present. Even a five-minute talk will elicit a "wow" reaction and an emotional bond when you're completely present. People around you believe they have your undivided attention and are the most important thing in the world to you right now.

Increased ability to be present enhances not only your body language, listening skills, and mental concentration, but it can also increase your ability to enjoy life. When a special occasion arises, such as a birthday party or even a few minutes of quality time with a loved one, our minds sometimes race in six directions.

We might hug a friend, but our calculations about how long to hug or what we'll say when we're finished obscure the warmth of our greeting. We go through the motions and are not fully present." Being fully present allows you to notice and enjoy the good moments fully.

You've just learned three quick fixes to use during interactions, and they'll become second nature with practice. Any time you get yourself back to full presence, keep that in mind that you reap significant benefits: you become more impactful, memorable, and grounded. You're laying the groundwork for a magnetic personality.

Let's look at the other two critical charisma qualities: strength and warmth, now that you know what presence is, why it matters to charisma, and how to get it.

WARMTH AND POWER

Being viewed as powerful implies having the ability to control or exert authority over others, whether by large sums of money, experience, intellect, sheer physical strength, or high social status. We search for signs of dominance in someone's presence, other people's reactions to them, and, most importantly, in their body language.

Simply put, warmth is goodwill for others. Warmth indicates if people would choose to use whatever influence they have to their advantage. Warmth can be described as being compassionate, altruistic, loving, or able to make a positive impact on our planet. Warmth is measured more explicitly than control, almost exclusively by body language and actions.

How do we determine the strength and warmth of a person? Consider the following scenario:

How do we determine the strength and warmth of a person? Assume you're meeting someone for the very first time. Most of the time, you don't have the luxury of conducting a thorough background check, conducting interviews with friends or family, or simply having the time to wait and observe their behaviour. As a result, you'll have to make a fast guess in the majority of cases.

We search for clues to measure warmth or strength in our experiences and change our assumptions accordingly. We presume riches when we see expensive clothes, polite body language when we see positive intentions, and a confident stance when we see someone who has something to feel confident about. In essence, whatever you project will be accepted by the majority of people.

You may increase your level of charisma simply by increasing your projection of power or warmth. However, you can really optimize your personal charisma ability if you can project both strength and warmth at the same time.

There are many ways to be seen as influential today, ranging from displaying intellect to displaying wealth. However, one mode of influence predominated in the early days of human history: brute force. Yes, information was valuable back then, but not nearly as much as it is now. Few people who rose to positions of power by brute strength and violence will be known for their warmth. In vital moments, the combination of power and warmth would have been extremely rare and extremely valuable: a strong figure who still treated us kindly may mean the difference between life and death. It has always been vital to our survival to figure out who would want to support us and who has the power to do so.

That's why we have such a strong reaction to power and warmth. We react to these qualities in the same way that we react to fat and sugar. Our ancestors lived by getting a strong positive response to fat and sugar—both of which helped our survival and were scarce in our original world. Despite the fact that they are plentiful today, our instinct remains. The same can be said about charisma: even though the mixture of warmth and strength is much easier to achieve nowadays, it still has a strong impact on our instincts. From lab tests to neuroimaging, research has repeatedly shown that they are the two dimensions we consider first and foremost when evaluating others.

Charisma necessitates the presence of both strength and warmth. Someone who is strong but not warm can be impressive, but they aren't often seen as charismatic, and they can come off as arrogant, cold, or distant. Warmth without control is likeable, but it isn't always viewed as charismatic, and it can come off as overeager, subservient, or desperate to please.

Though there are other approaches to charisma, the combination of presence, strength, and warmth is one of the most powerful mechanisms for maximizing charisma.

BODY LANGUAGE THAT IS ENTHUSIASTIC

Though it might seem unbelievable—how could words have so little weight as compared to the body language of the person delivering them? −it makes sense. Language is a relatively new discovery in the context of human evolution. But we've been communicating by nonverbal communication for a long time. As a result, nonverbal communication is much more deeply ingrained in our brains than our more recent language-processing skills. This is why nonverbal contact has such a strong influence.

Your body language is much more important than your vocabulary when it comes to charisma. You won't be charismatic if your body language is off, no matter how strong your message or how well-crafted your pitch is. On the other hand, you can be charming without saying anything if you use the right body language. It's always enough to project presence, influence, and warmth through your body language to be seen as charismatic.

CHARISMA IS A STATE OF MIND.

Were you conscious that your eyelids were fluttering in front of your eyes when you read the previous paragraph?

Isn't that correct? Despite this, they were blinking at regular intervals.

Have you ever noticed how heavy your tongue is in your mouth?

Or how are your toes positioned?

Have you forgotten about your eyelids once more?

Our bodies send out countless signals every minute without us even noticing it. These signs, including our breath and pulse, are among the millions of bodily functions regulated by our subconscious mind rather than our conscious mind. There is much too much nonverbal communication for us to be able to manage consciously.

This has two ramifications. First, we can't broadcast charismatic body language at will because we can't regulate all of our body languages. We'd have to simultaneously monitor thousands of things, from minute vocal variations to the precise degree and kind of stress around our eyes, to get all the signals right. It's virtually unthinkable. We won't be able to control charismatic body language. On the other hand, because our subconscious is in charge of the majority of our nonverbal signs, the problem will be solved if we could guide our subconscious in the right direction.

The second result is that, whether we like it or not, our body language reflects our mental state. Every second, our facial expressions, speech, stance, and all other aspects of body language represent our mental and emotional state. Since we don't actively regulate this flow, whatever is going on in our heads will manifest itself in our body language.

Even if we regulate our key facial expression or the way we hold our arms, legs, or head, if our internal state differs from what we're trying to convey, a microexpression will flash across our face sooner or later. Observers will note these split-second micro-expressions, even though they are brief (remember, people can read your face in as little as seventeen milliseconds). And if our main expression and that micro-expression are out of sync, people will sense it on a subconscious level: their intuition will tell them something isn't quite right.

Have you ever been able to tell the difference between a genuine and a fake smile? The difference between a social smile and a genuine smile is obvious. Two groups of facial muscles are involved in a genuine smile: one raises the corners of the mouth, while the other affects the region around the eyes. While the outer corners of the mouth raise in a sincere smile, the inner corners of the brows soften and fall down. Only the mouth corner muscle (the zygomatic major) is used in a fake smile. People can tell the difference because the smile does not reach the eyes, or at least not in the same way that a genuine smile would.

Since what is in your mind manifests in your body, and because people can notice even the tiniest micro expression, charismatic behaviours must originate in your mind in order to be efficient.

No amount of effort or willpower will compensate for an anti-charismatic internal state. Any of your deeper thoughts and emotions will emerge sooner or later. If your internal state is charismatic, on the other hand, the appropriate body language will emerge naturally. Thus, developing the different mental states that generate charismatic body language and behaviours is the first step in studying charisma, and this is what the first part of this book is all about.

We'll begin by learning about charismatic mental states: what they are, how to access them, and how to incorporate them so that they become second nature completely. We can only begin practising external charismatic behaviours after that. If you learn these skills in the wrong order, you could end up with embarrassing results. Assume you're delivering a critical presentation. You're doing fantastically well, using all of the fantastic new resources you've mastered and exuding an incredible amount of charisma. And, out of nowhere, someone says something that causes you to lose your mental concentration and your emotional trust. You lose all of your newly gained emotional confidence when you get flustered. You get flustered, and all of your newly developed abilities vanish.

Trying to improve your outward charisma while ignoring your internal environment is akin to putting pretty balconies on the house with a shaky base. It's a good touch, but everything falls apart after the first earthquake. It's difficult to recall, let alone use, the new skills you've just mastered if your internal state is in disarray. Internal charismatic skills, which help you manage your internal state, are the cornerstone upon which charismatic external skills are built.

Although charismatic people may have fewer technical skills than their peers, their internal and external skills provide them with a significant competitive advantage. Internal charisma skills provide both pieces of knowledge of one's own internal condition and the resources to handle it effectively.

YOUR BODY MANIFESTS WHAT YOUR MIND BELIEVES

Knowing the inner world begins with one main realization that underpins all charisma: the mind is incapable of distinguishing between reality and fiction. This is the one aspect of your inner world that can assist you in achieving the desired charismatic mental state almost instantly.

Have you ever had your heart race while watching a scary movie? You know it's just a movie, even if you don't realize it. You know you're watching actors who are happy to behave as if they're being killed in return for a good salary. However, when your brain sees blood and guts on the screen, it immediately goes into fight or flight mode, releasing adrenaline into your system. In reality, it goes like this:

Consider your favourite musical item.

Imagine the fingernails scraping over a chalkboard.

Consider dipping your hand into a bucket of sand and watching the grains crunch under your fingertips.

Now compare the sourness of lemon and lime. Which is sourer?

There was no sand, and there was no lemon to speak of. Despite this, your mind created very real physical responses in response to a series of entirely fictional events. Since your brain can't tell the difference between fantasy and reality, imaginary scenarios trigger your brain to send the same commands to your body as it does in a real situation. Your body will manifest whatever your mind believes. Simply putting yourself in a charismatic mental state can result in charismatic body language.

The placebo effect is a term used in medicine to describe the mind's powerfully beneficial effect on the body. A placebo is a simulated medical procedure in which patients are given "fake" pills and told they are getting real ones, or people are told they have received medical treatment when they haven't. Patients who receive these inert medications see a significant change in their medical condition in a surprising number of cases.

When drug supplies ran out during World War I, physicians learned that by convincing their patients that they had received pain-relieving medications, they could often alleviate their patients' misery. It gained widespread recognition in the 1950s when doctors started conducting supervised clinical trials. Throughout most of human history, most medicines were essentially placebo: physicians would prescribe potions or interventions that we now recognize to be profoundly ineffective. Despite this, people's health also improved as a result of the mind's remarkable ability to influence the body.

The placebo effect can be extremely strong at times. Many of the best charisma-boosting approaches are based on the placebo effect, and we'll talk about it a lot in this book. In reality, it's likely that you actually do this on a regular basis, and many of the techniques would make intuitive sense to you. We'll fine-tune this ability and make the internal processes you already use more efficient in the following chapters.

The nocebo effect, or mind-over-body effect, is a drawback of the mind-over-body effect. In this case, the mind induces harmful effects in the body as a result of entirely fictitious causes. Both the placebo and nocebo effects are essential in our ability to realize our charismatic potential fully. Since whatever is in our minds influences our bodies, and since our minds have difficulty distinguishing between imagination and reality, anything we imagine will influence our body language and, as a result, our charisma levels. Depending on the content of our imagination, it can significantly increase or decrease our charisma.

You've just learned the basis for several of the most effective internal charisma techniques, and we'll use them often.

CHAPTER THREE

THE OBSTACLES TO PRESENCE, POWER, AND WARMTH

Your ability to deliver charismatic body language is dependent on your mental state, as you now know. However, there are a variety of things that can — and sometimes do — get in the way of projecting presence, strength, or warmth. Knowing through internal barriers is currently impeding your personal charisma ability is the first step toward which your charisma. We'll look at the various types of physical and mental discomfort that can get in the way of your charismatic self in this chapter.

DISCOMFORT PHYSICALLY

Any physical distress that affects your noticeable, outward state — your body language — can influence how charismatic you are viewed. Assume that when you communicate with someone, he or she can sense (at least subconsciously) that whatever you do is related to him or her.

Physical pain has an effect not only on your external but also on your internal state. Hunger, for example, can affect your performance in a variety of ways. You may already be aware that when you're hungry, you think less clearly, or at least less clearly about things that aren't food-related. Low blood glucose levels have been linked to impaired attention, as well as problems controlling emotions and behaviour, according to numerous studies. This means you will find it more difficult to achieve the precise mental state needed for the charismatic actions you desire.

It's easy to get rid of physical pain that detracts from charisma:

1. Prevent
2. Recognize
3. Have a solution or explanation

The first and best step is to prepare ahead of time to avoid discomfort. In this case, the old adage "prevention is better than cure" remains true. Plan ahead as soon as possible to ensure your physical comfort. An easy way to make charisma easier to achieve is to keep this in mind while you make daily decisions.

When choosing a meeting place, think about how comfortable you would be. Take the temperature and noise level into account. Consider the temperature and volume of the environment. Make sure you're well-fed; if you're hosting, don't let yourself (or your guests) get too hungry. Consider your own energy level as well as the energy levels of the people you'll be engaging with. Is the meeting starting or ending very early or very late? People's body language will easily reveal signs of exhaustion as a lack of excitement.

Make sure you're dressed in clothes that won't make you too hot or too cold. Avoid itchy, ill-fitting, or otherwise distracting clothing. Any physical distraction will deplete part of your mental concentration and hinder your performance, even if you aren't aware of it. It's especially critical that your clothing is loose enough to allow you to breathe freely (this means you can take deep belly breaths, not shallow chest breaths). The amount of oxygen that gets to your brain, and hence how well you do mentally, is influenced by how well you breathe.

People can gain valuable confidence and, as a result, charisma by believing they look impressive even though their clothing is uncomfortable. It's up to you to determine if the pain is worth the boost of confidence. Wearing clothing that makes you feel both relaxed and secure in your appearance is ideal. Check and see if you're compromising comfort in tiny ways that are holding you back. Isn't it true that you're trying to gain whatever advantage you can?

The second step in coping with physical pain is to become aware of it. Check-in with your face every now and then to see if it's nervous. This is where your ability to remain present will come in handy once more: the more present you are, the more likely you are to notice if your body language is tense.

The third and final move is to act. If you notice that something is causing discomfort in your face, take action. Attempt to alleviate both the pain and the misinterpretation before others do so.

When you can't get rid of the physical pain, it's much more important to keep other people from taking the stress personally. Take a moment to clarify why you're in pain due to a specific problem. Explain the problem if, for example, you're annoyed by excessive nearby construction noise. Giving something a voice will usually encourage both of you to move on.

DISCOMFORT IN MIND

Psychological pain can manifest in our bodies as well as our minds, despite the fact that it originates entirely in mind. It has an effect on how we feel as well as how we are viewed. Anxiety, frustration, self-criticism, and self-doubt are all types of internal negativity that can limit our personal charisma capacity.

It's far more important to know how to deal with mental discomfort than it is to know how to deal with physical discomfort. This is both one of the most difficult and one of the most critical parts of the novel. It may be difficult to understand at first, but you will reap the benefits in the end. You'll be even more powerful as a result. You'll have acquired knowledge that will place you ahead of the game, and you'll have laid a base of knowledge on which the following parts will be built. So buckle up, take a deep breath, and keep reading.

UNCERTAINTY-INDUCED ANXIETY

Have you ever had the unsettling feeling that you're only waiting for the other shoe to drop and that you'd rather hear bad news than being kept guessing? Let's say you've recently begun a romantic relationship with someone, and they suddenly avoid answering your calls. They suddenly stop answering your calls, and your brain goes into overdrive. Your mind races through a list of alternative theories, obsessing about why they've stopped talking. Have you ever had the feeling that you'd rather get a firm "It's done" than never learn the reason for their silence? Even if the answer is a rejection, at least you will know. For all of us, being in a state of doubt or confusion is an unpleasant experience.

Our inability to cope with uncertainty has a number of consequences. It has the potential to lead to rash decisions. It can make us reveal more than we should in negotiations as we try to fill the silence, unable to bear the suspense of not understanding what the other person is thinking. Most importantly, it has the potential to make us feel nervous. Anxiety is a major flaw in charisma. First, it has an impact on our internal state: it's difficult to be completely present when you're nervous. Anxiety can also make us feel insecure. Anxiety, lack of presence, and lack of confidence can all manifest themselves in our body language, reducing our ability to radiate warmth.

If there's one thing we can count on, it's that confusion will persist. Given the rapid speed of business and technological advancements, as well as the unpredictable nature of economic upheavals, complexity and ambiguity will become a more prominent feature of our everyday lives. Those that are more adept at dealing with it would have a distinct advantage over their competitors.

Assume you're in the middle of a tough situation with an unpredictable result. You imagine a variety of scenarios and devise a strategy for dealing with each one. So far, all has gone well. After you've considered and scenario, the rational, sensible, and logical thing to do are to put the situation out of your mind and go about your business before action is needed.

But how many of us have experienced our minds running through the various outcomes repeatedly, rehashing the various plans we've made, replaying future scenarios, mentally rehearsing the forthcoming discussions not once or twice, but ad nauseam?

Another legacy of our survival instincts is our innate aversion to confusion. We are more at ease with what we are familiar with, which has clearly not killed us yet, than with what is unfamiliar or unclear, which could prove to be dangerous.

It's worthwhile to learn how to deal with uncertainty, not just because it boosts charisma but also because the ability to deal with complexity and uncertainty is one of the best predictors of business performance.

Just a few business schools teach students how to deal with confusion. Psychologists, on the other hand, have been helping people improve their expertise in this area for decades, developing and improving techniques specifically for this purpose.

The liability shift is the single most successful strategy I've discovered for reducing the discomfort of ambiguity. What we just want to hear in unpredictable circumstances is that everything will turn out well. The confusion would be far less stressful if we knew everything would work out—that all would be taken care of. Please take a few moments to try out the workout.

1. Relax and close your eyes while sitting comfortably or lying down.
2. Take a couple of deep breaths. Imagine pulling clean air into the top of your head when you inhale. Allow the air to rush through you as you exhale, washing away all worries and concerns.
3. Choose a benevolent entity—God, Fate, the Universe, whatever fits your values best—and imagine it.
4. Visualize the weight of everything you're worried about—this meeting, this interaction, this day—being lifted off your shoulders and placed on the shoulders of whatever person you've chosen. They've taken over.
5. Visually take something off your shoulders and feel the difference, knowing that you are no longer in control of the outcome of any of these events. All has been taken care of for you. You should sit back, relax, and take in whatever good fortune you come across.
6. Pay careful attention the next time you find yourself contemplating different outcomes to a situation. Try a burden shift to relieve some of the pressure if your mind is spinning in circles, obsessing about potential outcomes. Consider the possibility of an all-powerful entity—the Universe, God, Fate—to whom you may entrust all your worries.

So, how did it turn out for you? Did you have any physical repercussions as a result of your actions? Many people experience feeling lighter or their chests opening up and widening after transferring responsibility. If you didn't have any physical or emotional reactions, it's possible that the confusion was not causing you any distress. If you sensed something, congratulations: you've just completed a liability transition.

Many people have found themselves referring to this approach so often that it has become second nature to them. It becomes easier to imagine, pass their daily worries and cares, and enjoy the physiological results of the transfer with each practice.

The reason this approach works is that our brain's first response when faced with a scenario, is to accept it as realistic.

"Our brains are wired to understand first, believe second, and disbelieve third. We start with the physiological effects since disbelief necessitates extra cognitive effort. And, although this conviction can only last a fraction of a second, it is sufficient to produce emotional and physical reassurance, which can alter our thinking patterns and help relieve unpleasant feelings." Visuals affect our physiology well before cognitive disbelief sets in. Visuals often bypass our cognitive circuits and go directly to our emotional levels in the brain.

The transition of liability does not eliminate confusion (the outcome remains uncertain). Instead, it exacerbates the situation (the outcome remains uncertain). Rather, it makes the confusion more bearable. This distinction is important. People can go to great lengths to alleviate the fear caused by confusion, including making hasty decisions, forcing bad results, and numbing their anxiety with a variety of mind-altering drugs. The obligation transition, on the other hand, functions without attempting to eliminate confusion. Instead, it aids you in being less affected by it, pulling you out of the negative mental and physical states that often surround a state of uncertainty. Your situation's outcome may still be unpredictable, but you're no longer concerned about it.

You're putting to use the wonderful placebo effect—the brain's inability to differentiate between imagination and reality—by presenting the mind with the possibility that responsibility has been shifted. The placebo effect works even though we realize we're deceiving ourselves, as we'll see in later chapters, possibly due to this inherent cognitive delay in disbelief.

Perform a fast visualization to pass liability if you notice your anxiety level is rising. It's incredible to feel the immediate sense of relief, as well as the rising comfort, peace, and serenity. You will note that your whole body begins to relax and glow at times.

COMPARISON-BASED DISSATISFACTION

Assume you're at a big dinner party of guests seated at various tables. In stark contrast to the previous party you attended, which was a lot of fun, the talk at your table is very boring. To make matters worse, laughter erupts from the table next to you. Isn't it normal to say to yourself, "I wish I were at that other table?" They seem to be having a lot more fun...?

Humans are compelled to compare by accident. We prefer to equate our current experiences to our past experiences, to the experiences of others, or to our ideal vision of what an experience should be whenever we have one. This tendency also becomes the experience itself. When we are faced with several choices and try to make the best decision possible in order to maximize the result, this tendency becomes even more pronounced.

Our charisma is harmed at every point of this cycle. Our desire to be completely present is hampered by the process of contrasting and judging. Trying to maximize both detracts from our involvement and causes anxiety as a result of the need to make the best decision possible. And a negative assessment can easily lead to negative emotions like disappointment, jealousy, or anger.

Trying to overcome this desire to compare is difficult because it is deeply ingrained in our brains. Instead, pay attention to whether you're making comparisons and use the burden shift strategy to relieve any internal pressure.

SELF-CRITICISM

Assume you're on your way to a critical review. When the time for the test comes, the critical inner voice assaults you with self-doubt, recalling previous mistakes, humiliations, and inadequacies. Anxiety levels increase, and if you don't know how to manage the physical side effects of your internal critic's assault, your performance will suffer. (Don't worry, you'll learn what you need to deal with episodes.)

Few items have a greater effect on people's success than their self-esteem. Athletes will tell you that no matter how physically trained they are, a poor mental condition will impair their results. Negative emotions may have real-life physical effects.

It can feel like we're being attacked when our internal voice begins to criticize and lash out at us. Since our brain can't tell the difference between fantasy and fact, these internal threats are interpreted by our mind as if they were a real physical attack, and they can trigger the threat response, also known as the fight-or-flight response.

The consequences of this activation are well-documented. When a zebra is chased by a lion, the human body releases adrenaline and cortisol (stress hormones) into the bloodstream, directing all of its energy to vital functions such as increased heart and breathing rates, muscle response, vision acuity, and so on. The body is more concerned with surviving ten more minutes than with living ten more years. Non-essential functions like muscle repair, digestion, and the immune system, as well as "superfluous" functions like logical reasoning, are turned off. To put it another way, intelligent thought is turned off because it isn't necessary for survival.

Let's pretend you're having a chat. You say something and then think to yourself, "Oh, that was a dumb thing to say." What will happen to your appearance? Your face may tense as you wince at the thought. Since we can't regulate our body language, any negativity in our minds will inevitably show up on our faces, as we've mentioned.

The negative expression, no matter how fleeting, will be noticed by the person in front of you. And all they know is that you had a sour smile on your face when staring at them and listening to them. They'll naturally think your gesture was a reaction to them—what they said or did or what you thought of them. This is how, in addition to your performance, internal negativity influences your body language and thus your charisma.

One of the most popular roadblocks to great success in any area is self-criticism. Since so many executives suffer from it and so few dare to speak out about it, it's often referred to as the silent killer of industry.

DOUBTS ABOUT ONESELF

Simply put, self-doubt is a lack of belief in one's own ability to do something: we doubt our ability to do it or our ability to learn how to do it. Worse, it's the feeling that we're missing something crucial, something important but unattainable, and that we're simply not good enough. An impostor syndrome is a form of self-doubt in which competent people believe they don't really know what they're doing and are just waiting for someone to expose them as a fraud. Surprisingly, high performers are the ones who suffer the most from impostor syndrome.

Anxiety, disappointment, self-criticism, and self-doubt have all been observed. What is the source of all this negativity? The negative emotions we have are an inevitable byproduct of one of our most important survival mechanisms. Negativity exists to motivate you to take action, either to solve the dilemma or to get out of it. Fear and anxiety are intended to motivate you to take action. They're inconvenient because they're "made" to be inconvenient.

There are moments when the pain of full-fledged terror is absolutely necessary. If we were at imminent physical risk, we would undoubtedly appreciate our bodies directing all of their energies into ensuring our short-term survival. In today's world, however, only a few conditions warrant a complete fight-or-flight response. Our instinctive responses actually work against us in these situations.

Have you ever been paralyzed in the middle of a test or suffered from stage fright? You freeze, your pulse races, and your palms sweat like a deer in headlights. You're frantically attempting to recall what you intended to say or do, but your mind is blank. Your higher cognitive functions are no longer functioning.

When we're stressed, our minds believe we're in a fight-or-flight situation, declare a state of emergency, and shut down what it considers to be unnecessary functions. Unfortunately, this means that our cognitive capacities are deteriorating right as we need them the most. Though it may be difficult to remember in the middle of an anxiety attack, rest assured that this is a perfectly normal, natural reaction that was designed to benefit your health.

Of course, a healthy dose of self-doubt will motivate us to take action. The impostor syndrome, for example, can be a powerful motivator, encouraging us to work harder than anyone else. But how much would it cost? Given that internal negativity affects our body language and therefore our relationships, as well as our ability to enjoy life, isn't it easier to learn how to deal with the impostor syndrome and be driven more by trust in our abilities and the joy of accomplishment?

Understanding how to deal with impostor syndrome and the inner critic It's crucial to understand how to deal with impostor syndrome and your inner critic if you want to maximize your charisma. You can get some distance from internal negativity with practice, using strategies like the ones you'll learn in the next chapter, and even get to a point where the inner critic's voice elicits just a smile or a chuckle from you.

So far, you've learned about internal negativity, how to recognize it, and how it manifests itself in your mind and body. In the next chapter, you'll learn how to put your newfound knowledge into action.

CHAPTER FOUR

OVERCOMING THE OBSTACLES

You've already gained valuable knowledge about how physical and mental discomfort can limit your personal charisma. In this chapter, you'll learn how to put your newfound knowledge into action, overcome challenges, and effectively deal with almost any internal discomfort. You'll be able to comfortably manage any uncomfortable feelings that emerge, including self-doubt, impatience, frustration, and irritation.

Destigmatize pain, neutralize negativity, and rewrite truth are three steps to successfully managing any difficult encounter. Let's get this party started.

TO BEGIN, TAKE THE FIRST STEP. DISCOMFORT SHOULD BE DE-STIGMATIZED.

Destigmatizing an event simply means recognizing that it is natural, ordinary, and nothing to be concerned about or ashamed of. Internal dissatisfaction and negativity are a normal part of existence. It happens to everybody.

Nonetheless, we've developed the habit of taking any physical or mental discomfort as a sign of something amiss, maybe even a sign of something wrong inside us, in our society. And when we tolerate a certain amount of sorrow or distress during unsettling life events—

major career shifts, divorce, the loss of a loved one—we also set a time limit on the acceptability of our emotions, during which we conclude that continuing to feel this way will be unacceptable.

One of the biggest reasons we have a hard time dealing with negative feelings, emotions, and internal interactions is that we believe they "shouldn't" be happening. As a result, we not only feel bad, but we also feel bad about feeling bad.

To de-stigmatize, remind yourself that whatever your internal distress is, it's a normal part of the human experience and a product of one of our brain's survival mechanisms. It can help to think of those who have been through what you are going through, particularly if you can think of someone who is similar to you but a step or two ahead of you—someone you can relate to and respect.

If you've recently lost the main client, consider someone you know—a mentor you admire or a colleague you admire—who has experienced a similar setback. Consider how they would feel if they went through this. Of course, hearing them tell you their story in person is perfect, but even just picturing them going through this or telling you about it can be beneficial. (Keep in mind that your brain won't be able to tell the difference.)

Reminding yourself that you're not alone with your discomfort is another way to de-stigmatize it. With about 7 billion people on the planet, not just one, but thousands of people are experiencing the same thing right now. Rather than viewing it as a single large emotion experienced by a single individual, see it as a group of people dealing with a daunting burden shared by many. Rather than seeing the problem as yours alone to bear, see it as the depression, guilt, and sorrow that many people are experiencing right now.

Shame, you see, is the true murderer. It is one of the most harmful to one's wellbeing and happiness of all the feelings that one can experience. Shame has such an effect on us because it sends a message about our basic acceptability as human beings. In terms of life, if the tribe refuses you, you will perish. It's a life-or-death scenario. The brain associates social needs with survival; hunger and rejection elicit identical neural responses. The fear of being so despised that we are rejected by those who matter to our survival lurks somewhere in the back of our minds.

Shame can rapidly develop out of proportion and manifest in ways that aren't beneficial to us because it's easily activated and escalates.

Charisma requires the ability to eliminate the stigma of guilt from painful feelings and experiences. It's not really what we're feeling that's the most painful—it's guilt about feeling this way that causes the most damage. It becomes much easier to bear this feeling once we accept it as natural and even anticipated. It's important to note that shame is a normal part of the human experience and that everyone experiences it from time to time.

Try this step-by-step guide to destigmatizing the next time an unpleasant emotion bothers you:

1. Recognize that unpleasant feeling are common, inevitable, and simply a result of our evolutionary survival instincts. They happen to all of us from time to time.
2. Dedramatize: this is a normal aspect of human life that occurs on a daily basis.
3. Consider those who have gone through similar situations in the past, especially people you admire.
4. View it as a responsibility that is shared by many people. You are a member of a group of people who are all experiencing the same emotion at the same time.

What you've just discovered is how to de-stigmatize internal distress, allowing you to be more resilient to charisma-damaging negativity. You've also increased your charisma level by acquiring these resources. These are essential resources that you'll use in the rest of the book.

Step 2: Get Rid of Negativity

The next step in dealing with internal negativity is to neutralize negative feelings after you've de-stigmatized the experience. The right way to do this is to acknowledge that your opinions aren't always right.

And when it seems that someone is responding negatively to us, the expression on their face could be unrelated to us. What's going on behind our backs that we can't see? Is it because they're hungry, sick, or tired? Perhaps they're suffering from an emotional or physical ailment that they're unable to overcome.

Try to note that the next time you notice coldness or reservation in someone's face when they're talking to you, it might just be the overt manifestations of their internal discomfort. It's possible that you're catching the surface tremors of an internal storm, and it has nothing to do with how they feel about you or what you've just said.

One of the key reasons we're so influenced by our negative thinking is that we believe our minds have a good grip on truth and that their assumptions are generally right. This, on the other hand, is a fallacy. Our perception of truth in our minds can be, and often is, totally skewed.

Look around the room right now and find all that is blue.

Keep your gaze fixed on this page now. Consider everything in the room that is red without raising your eyes.

It's true. Please bear with me. Give it all you've got.

Now take a look around. Do you see a lot of red lately?

What caused this to happen? Our capacity for conscious attention is restricted, limiting how much we can be aware of at any given moment. We actively experience only a small percentage of the millions of visual inputs our eyes receive every second. It would be exhausting to be fully aware of all that is going on around us.

To cope with this, our brain searches for relevant information—either what it considers significant or what we've asked it to pay attention to. Our mind does not give us a complete and accurate portrayal of truth as a result of this process. Since it has to filter, it presents us with an incomplete image, displaying only some elements while hiding the rest.

Most of the time, the missing elements don't matter, and the image we get is pretty accurate. However, our minds may often present us with a severely skewed perception of reality. And since the components that our danger-focused brain considers significant are typically the most negative, the distortion is often negative. The negativity bias is the term for this tendency.

Remind yourself that you might not be having an accurate view of reality as your mind spins pessimistic scenarios. Your brain might be succumbing to its negativity bias, emphasizing certain elements more than others, or completely ignoring some positives.

Similar to how an optical illusion tricks your eyes into seeing objects that aren't there, your mind can be fooled by thinking illusions that make you believe a false belief is true.

Imagine strolling along the mind's pathways. Suddenly, you become aware of a negative feeling. Consider it as a piece of wall graffiti. That's all it is, graffiti—not it's a judgment of your character.

Thoughts can also be seen on the surface of your mind as flickers of electricity crackling. Thoughts, on the other hand, are nothing more than electrical impulses transmitted from one part of your brain to another.

View your continent, then your nation, region, and finally, the room in which you are.

- Imagine your tiny self, electrical impulses whizzing through your brain. At this precise moment, one small being has a unique experience.
- Consider your mental chatter as a clock; see if you can lower the volume or simply place the radio to the side and let it blare away.
- Think of the worst-case scenario with your situation. Recognize that no matter what happens, you will succeed. Consider how many occasions you've felt like this before— like you wouldn't make it through—and yet you did.

We're learning how to silence unhelpful thoughts here. We don't want to fall into the pit of arguing with them or attempting to control them.

Since attempting to remove a self-critical thought just serves to reinforce it, it's much easier to strive to neutralize it simply.

Destigmatizing distress and neutralizing negativity are the first two steps in dealing with internal negativity. The third and final move will assist you in not only reducing internal negativity but also in replacing it with a new internal truth.

Step three is the most important. Rewrite the Facts

It's 8:00 a.m. on a Monday morning, and you're on your way to a crucial meeting on the freeway. You'll be offering a thirty-minute presentation that has the potential to change your career path. You're relaxed and concentrated. A big black car suddenly cuts in front of you, swerving into your path. You stomp on the brake with your heart racing and your hands clutching the steering wheel. This car not only cut in front of you without signalling, but it's also speeding up and down erratically, almost causing you to rear-end it. Then it swerves back into your path, making the tires on the car to your right screech. What a moron, irresponsible pilot! Your veins are throbbing with anger.

What happened to your body as a result of this? Your heart rate accelerated, your muscles tightened, and stress hormones flooded your bloodstream as a result of the fight-or-flight response. You're now filled with anxiety and anger. You know you need to return to a charismatic mental and physical condition in time for your presentation, but you just have a few minutes and can't get that fool driver out of your head.

It's difficult to calm down once the fight-or-flight response has been triggered. Anger is a difficult emotion to let go of, which is why a bad traffic experience in the morning will linger in your mind for hours, if not all day.

You'd pay a high price if all you wanted to do were suppress your rage. When people are triggered into a negative emotional state and then asked to suppress negative feelings, their internal negative experience always remains unchanged, and their brain and cardiovascular system experience elevated stress responses.

What if you discovered that this ostensibly reckless driver was really a terrified mother whose baby was choking in the backseat, and she was desperately trying to pull over into the breakdown lane while reaching back to save her baby's life?

Will that make you feel less enraged right away?

It will work for the vast majority of people.

The brain's tension levels are effectively reduced when you decide to alter your belief in what happened (technically known as cognitive reappraisal).

We don't know for sure what motivates a person's behaviour in most cases, so we may as well take the most helpful theory and construct a version of events that puts us in the mental state we need for charisma.

Though this idea may seem irrational at first, rewriting your view of truth is the logical and intelligent thing to do. It will assist you in regaining the mental state necessary to exude charismatic body language while also improving your performance.

So, rather than attempting to mask or disregard your internal problems when a traumatic encounter occurs that threatens to impair your charisma levels, consider a few alternate versions of reality.

Conjure up a few situations that will help you achieve a more useful mental state. Naturally, the most useful alternate universe isn't always the most enjoyable.

The most important questions are: Which mental state will be most beneficial in this situation? And in this case, which version of the truth will be more useful? And which version of the truth will assist you in achieving your goal? When a situation challenges your level of warmth or trust, you may use this strategy to boost your charisma. Simply imagining a different reason for a trivial incident is always enough to alleviate frustration or impatience and replace it with compassion. Assume you're late for an important meeting due to traffic, and your anxiety levels are rising. Consider this: What if the delay is beneficial? Rep the question a few times to see how inventive the mind becomes in its responses. It might come up with reasons like this:

- If traffic had normally been moving, my route might have crossed that of an eighteen-wheel truck skidding through the intersection.

- The people I'm meeting are working under a tight deadline and are thankful for every minute I'm late because it helps them to work a little longer.
- The Universe (or Fate or God), who cares for my well-being, does not want this meeting to take place. Instead, things will go in a far better direction.

Look down and type out a new reality on a sheet of paper while you're dealing with a more serious case. Writing has the ability to reach various parts of our brain and influence our views in ways that other forms of speech do not. Committing things to paper has been shown to be crucial in both changing people's minds and making imaginary stories seem more tangible. "The speech is going well..." write in the present tense. Alternatively, use the past tense: "The speech was a total triumph..."

You may need to be charismatic against someone you despise at times. As you would expect, anger is an unappealing mental state that manifests itself in a high level of negativity in both your mind and your body language. Furthermore, the effects of bringing this negativity around are felt by your body. "Resentment is like drinking poison and waiting for the other person to die," says one of my favourite adages.

You should keep your internal discomfort from messing with your charisma no matter what the circumstances of your anger are. However, getting rid of resentment isn't easy. When this happens, rewriting the truth can be extremely beneficial. One good way to relieve resentment is to do the exercise below. This can be both the most uncomfortable and the most satisfying of all the truth rewriting exercises you do.

- Consider a person in your life who has harmed you.

- Take a blank page and write a letter to that person, telling them what you wish you had told them. Put your heart and soul into this—you have nothing to lose. Make a point of writing it out by hand.

- Set the letter aside until you've taken it off your mind and onto paper.

- Take a new sheet of paper and write their answer exactly how you want them to respond. You should make them accept responsibility for their decisions, admitting and apologizing for everything they've ever done to cause you pain. You don't need to justify their actions; what you need are an acknowledgement and an apology. Since it's your imagination, you can choose just what you want to hear.

For many people, this exercise will feel strange, uncomfortable, or surreal at first. It's also possible that you won't notice any internal changes right away. However, you may be surprised to feel this "modern fact" gradually taking root over the next few days. You may believe that you have received the closure you sought. Simply reread the apology letter every night for a few days to speed up the process. You'll be pleased with the outcome.

You can choose your view of the situation by using these two exercises, rewriting reality and getting satisfaction, which allows you to be both successful and charismatic.

Putting All Together

Let's bring it all together now that you've mastered the three-step method for overcoming internal barriers to charisma. The following example will show you how the series works in real life. It contains guidelines for destigmatizing pain, neutralizing negativity, and rewriting truth that you can use at any time.

Getting Used to Being Uncomfortable

You've really come a long way. You've learned an array of strategies to help you conquer the most common barriers to charisma since the beginning of this chapter. However, there is one more thing you must learn. If you want to hit advanced charisma stages, where the masters work, you'll need the next tool. No matter how complicated your internal situation is, this approach will help you reclaim your charisma. It's like getting a hidden weapon up your sleeve. Knowing it'll be there for you when and where you need it will give you a strong sense of security.

This technique can give you an advantage in negotiations, presentations, and social situations—in fact, anywhere where your success is important. It is, however, a difficult tool to master because it necessitates going against the most primitive instincts. So, what is this mysterious weapon? Being at ease in the presence of discomfort.

Does it seem to be straightforward? Yes, it is. Simple, but not without difficulty.

Focusing on this minor sensation of your physical pain accomplishes a dual goal: it gives your mind something meaningful to concentrate on other than its increasing conviction that this situation is untenable. It also has the benefit of immediately getting you into full presence, which is a key component of charisma. In reality, delving into sensations is a technique that can help you access charismatic presence even in the most challenging circumstances.

CHAPTER FIVE

CREATING CHARISMATIC MENTAL STATES

In the subsequent chapter, you learned how to manage the most popular celebrity-inhibiting obstacles skillfully. You're now in a position to cultivate the mental states that will enable you to achieve your full charisma potential. You'll learn how to boost your morale and exude warmth and strength, which are two of the three main components of charisma. You'll also learn how to build any mental state you need, from tranquillity to victory.

THE USE OF VISUALIZATION

"Imagining oneself performing an operation stimulates parts of the brain that are used in actually performing the activity," says one researcher. This is why visualization is so effective—in reality, and some athletes claim to be physically exhausted after intensive visualization sessions. Visualization can also affect the structure of the brain: studies have shown that actually imagining yourself playing the piano enough times causes a detectable and measurable change in the motor cortex of the brain.

The brain is an adaptable organ that is continually rewiring itself. The previously held belief that it becomes fixed in its ways after a certain age has now been proved to be significantly incorrect. We fire those neuronal connections while we use our brain, and the more we use them, the stronger they become. We're actually rubbing grooves into our brains, and any mental mechanisms we use on a regular basis will become stronger. Whatever mental tendencies you concentrate on can be built and then strengthened.

Method acting arose to assist actors in achieving their most daunting goal: perfecting their body language. Trying to manipulate as much of their body language as possible was frustrating and futile: even with years of practice, it's difficult to control the flow fully. If their emotions internally were not what they wanted the outside world to see, their underlying thoughts and feelings would eventually surface.

Method acting, on the other hand, took a different approach. Rather than making people attempt to manipulate their body language, it went straight to the source—the mind—and made the actors aspire to become the characters they were aiming to portray so that they could really experience the feelings they wanted to express. The thousands of body language signals would then flow in a normal and consistent manner.

Visualization is one of the most important charisma-boosting techniques available because of its strong mental and physiological effects. The right visualization will help you boost both your internal sense of trust and your ability to project it outward. Your subconscious mind can send a remarkable chain reaction of trust signals cascading through your body simply by using the right mental images. In reality, by choosing the right visualization, you can view almost any type of body language.

A step-by-step guide to visualization is given below, which you can use anytime you want to alter your internal state. You'll practice visualizing trust here, but there are also exercises for visualizing comfort and empathy, as well as relaxation and serenity, later in the book.

The visualization that follows is a perfect way to boost the amount of power you want to express. You can do this exercise on the couch at home, at work sitting at your desk, or even in an elevator—anywhere you have a minute to close your eyes.

- Relax by closing your eyes.
- Consider a time when you were fully satisfied.
- Triumphant—for instance, the day you won a competition or an award.
- Hear the murmurs of approval and the swell of applause in the room.
- Observe people's smiles and soft and admiring expressions.
- Feel the congratulatory handshakes and your feet on the deck.
- Above all, be aware of your emotions and the warm glow of trust that arises within you.

Do you have more self-assurance now? Some people get immediate results from their first visualization, while others don't. Your ability to construct realistic visualizations will improve with practice, just like any other skill.

Thinking in a visualization scenario is easy for some people. Others, on the other hand, are more sensitive to auditory cues, so here's an alternative to visualization: mentally concentrate on key phrases.

These axioms can come in handy in times of panic when our minds go blank, and all we can recall are a few basic phrases. Beginner white-water rafters are given a simple rhyme to remember—"toes to nose"—to remind them of the sequence of moves they should perform if the boat tips over. Also, seasoned firefighters have been known to rely on a slogan like "Put the white stuff on the red stuff" to motivate them during a burn.

Actual sensory feedback can also be added to the visualizations. Play music as you verbalize or subvocalize, for example, and choose songs that make you feel particularly energized and optimistic.

If you really want to go all out, add movement to your visualizations to take them to the next level. Since physiology influences psychology (yes, your body influences your mind), certain gestures or postures can elicit specific emotions.

Consider what gesture you make when you accomplish something, such as a good golf shot or when you receive particularly good news. Is it a traditional fist pump? Alternatively, you may lift your arms in the air and exclaim, "YES!" By including this gesture (and any accompanying words, if applicable) at the end of your visualization, when your optimism is at its peak, you'll engage your entire physiology and "lock-in" the victorious feeling, enhancing the exercise's impact.

Keep refining all of these dimensions—visual, auditory, and kinesthetic—as you move. If you think a certain picture, expression, action, or song works well, try changing it up a little and seeing how it affects the outcome. When you zoom in on visual images, sounds, or feelings, notice what happens. Continue to make little improvements, whether you hear positive voices or feel the warmth of the sun. Over the years, the mix of sights and sounds that work best for me has evolved significantly.

Visualization is a genuinely miraculous technique for boosting morale, radiating more warmth, replacing fear with relaxed serenity, or accessing whatever emotion you want to experience and then broadcasting it through your body language. To effectively help you restore composure and belief, it's worth taking the time to build and practice a go-to visualization. That way, you won't have to come up with new imagery on the fly when you're stressed. With new imagery on the move, you'll always know what works. You'll always be aware of what works best for you.

Here are three more visualizations to use before making a presentation, attending an important meeting, or if you're feeling nervous.

Just before giving a presentation: Some of the most well-known speakers of this century claim to have used some kind of visualization just before taking the stage. It would be rare to come across a fantastic speaker who does not.

To get the most out of your visualization, arrive early at the venue so you can walk around the stage and get a feel for the room. You can also bring the appropriate music with you and begin the visualizations right on stage, with the aim of associating confident, victorious feelings with being in that specific setting. Try to make mental movies when listening to an upbeat, energizing soundtrack, vividly imagining how well the speech is going, seeing and hearing the audience's positive reaction as you confidently walk around the stage.

BEFORE A CRUCIAL MEETING:

One of the keys to great success is visualization. Imagine the smiles they have on their faces because they enjoyed you and are trusting in the value you are giving them" before important meetings. You can imagine as much detail as you want, including seeing the lines around their eyes when they smile." Visualize the whole conversation, right down to the firm handshakes that end the meeting and seal the deal.

If your message needs to convey warmth, compassion, or empathy, for example, getting yourself into a warm and empathetic state will make it much easier to find the right words. Visualizing a scene that evokes these emotions, such as a young child coming to tell you about her school problems, will help your mind prepare for the right language to flow.

When you're feeling nervous, flooding your brain with oxytocin is the most effective way to make you feel better. The fight-or-flight response's arousal is immediately reversed. The fight-or-flight response's arousal is immediately reversed.

Visualization is an extremely useful technique. This is the technique to make a permanent part of your toolkit out of all the charisma-boosting techniques. This one strategy, if you take nothing else away from this book, will make a significant difference in your charisma.

COMPASSION, GRATITUDE, AND GOODWILL

One of the most important aspects of charismatic activity is warmth. It has the potential to make others like you trust you and want to support you. Warmth isn't an obvious or convenient feeling for many people; it just doesn't come naturally to them.

Many of us find it difficult to stay warm. This may be due to a variety of factors, including birth, childhood, current circumstances, or simply personality. To feel warm, you must use every tool in this book, including the one you're about to learn. From the last person to the most personal, there will be a three-step incremental progression into warmth.

The first step is to connect with feelings of warmth toward life in general and your life in particular. This comes under the heading of appreciation in general. For those of us who find it difficult to communicate with others, gratitude has a distinct benefit. It can provide us with charismatic warmth without requiring us to interact with others.

Then you'll try out warmth for others—this is where goodwill, altruism, sympathy, and empathy come into play.

Finally, you'll look at what most of us consider to be the least pleasurable kind of warmth: warmth for yourself. Self-compassion is a new discipline that is gaining popularity.

All of these will give you a noticeable boost in charisma, so try out all of them if you can, both the natural ones and the ones that are a stretch.

Gratitude and Appreciation are the first steps.

What exactly is the polar opposite of gratitude? Resentment, neediness, and desperation are not charismatic emotions. We all know that giving off the feeling of desperation will ruin someone's chances, whether they're on a job interview or on a date. Gratitude is an excellent solution to all of these negative emotions because it stems from appreciating what you already have—from material possessions to meaningful relationships. Gratitude can be a powerful charisma conduit, taking you back to the present moment and providing instant access to feelings of trust and warmth.

These days, everybody seems to be preaching thanks. The research, as well as the ways in which gratitude will increase your charisma, is convincing. If you can access gratitude, your entire body language can change in an instant: your smile will soften, and your entire body will relax. People will find your body language to be really attractive because it will exude both warmth and grounded confidence.

However, few of us have the ability actually to choose to be grateful. Gratitude isn't easy for the majority of people. Humans are hardwired for hedonic adaptation or the propensity to take our good fortune for granted. It's also futile to tell yourself that you should be thankful because it just brings up guilt.

Focusing on little items that are physically real is one way to evoke a sense of appreciation. Another good way to boost your appreciation is to look at your life from a third-person perspective and write a meaningful story about yourself.

The act of writing has a significant impact on the exercise's success. It gives the optimistic outlook more weight and substance. If you simply imagine how someone else sees your life, it may not feel genuine, and its substance and weight may be lost. If you write it down, even if it feels strange at first, it will feel strangely real by the end of the paragraph.

STEP 2: COMPASSION AND GOODWILL

Have you ever been with someone that you knew genuinely cared for your well-being? How did that make you feel? You most definitely had fun, warm feelings. Goodwill is a powerful tool for both projecting warmth and instilling warmth in others. When you genuinely care for someone's well-being, you feel more connected to them, it reflects on your face, and others see you as a warm person—your charisma level skyrockets.

Goodwill is the next step on the path to comfort and, eventually, charisma. Goodwill can immediately infuse your body language with more warmth, empathy, caring, and compassion—all of which are very charismatic qualities.

Goodwill boosts your mood by flooding your system with positive energy. Goodwill makes you feel better by flooding the brain with the feel-good chemicals oxytocin and serotonin. Furthermore, it reduces our desire to make the interaction a success in a fascinating way. When our sole goal is to spread goodwill, the burden is relieved. We're no longer striving, struggling, or moving things in a particular direction. We can both project and feel more charismatic trust because we're less worried about how the interaction goes.

The simple act of wishing someone well is known as goodwill. It's similar to a mental muscle that can be improved with practice. You should retrain the goodwill muscles even though they've been atrophied.

Finding three things you like about the person you want to feel good about is an easy but successful way to start. Find three things to admire or approve of whoever you're speaking with, even if it's as simple as "their shoes are shined" or "they were on time." When you begin looking for positive aspects, your mental state shifts, which is reflected in your body language.

More intensive goodwill exercises are mentioned below for you to try. They work immediately for certain people. Others find them strange. Simply check them out; if they don't fit for you, we'll have more for you to try.

First, a mental image. This will assist you in changing your viewpoint. If you can see someone as a genuinely good person, even for a split second, your emotional response to them will soften and warm, changing your whole body language. So give it a shot: see people with angel wings walking and driving when you're out walking or driving. It's also a good idea to see yourself with wings. Imagine that you're all part of a team of angels who are all doing their very best.

Try a few different phrases if you respond better to auditory guides. Consider this: when looking at someone, think to yourself, "I like you." And I like you for who you are. Alternatively, try remembering this rule: Love as much as you can from wherever you are. Remind yourself of these maxims many times a day, and remember how your mind and body can change. Another common saying is: Of all the choices available to me right now, which one will carry the most love into the world?

These three strategies may be all that is required for some people to feel goodwill and, as a result, charisma-enhancing warmth. For them, merely concentrating on wishing others well is enough to bring warmth into their lives. It may not be enough for some. Perhaps the individual to whom we wish to extend goodwill is a sourpuss. Cantankerousness is something we'd like to express goodwill against. It's possible that we're irritated or resentful of them. Or maybe they're just too far away.

In these situations, consider moving a step further and expressing empathy and compassion.

• Goodwill implies that you wish everyone well even though you don't know how they're feeling.

• Empathy means you understand what they're going through; perhaps you've had a similar experience before. Compassion is empathy combined with goodwill: you realize what they're going through and wish them well.

The following is the order in which compassion is accessed: first, empathy, or the ability to recognize and sense suffering in others; second, sympathy, or being emotionally moved by distress; and third, compassion, or the urge to care for the well-being of the distressed individual.

The good news is that we are born with a natural proclivity for compassion; it is deeply ingrained in our minds, even more so than cognitive ability.

Everything you need to change your body language is a desire to reflect on the well-being of others. This will suffice to give people the impression that you really care for them, and it is one of the most important characteristics of charisma.

Swimming is how you learn to swim. And, even though it feels uncomfortable at first, you learn to be compassionate by practising compassion.

STEP THREE IS THE MOST IMPORTANT. COMPASSION FOR ONESELF

To begin, let's define three main concepts:

Our trust in our ability to do or learn anything is referred to as self-confidence.

The amount of approval or importance we place on ourselves is referred to as self-esteem. It's frequently a comparison-based assessment (whether measured against other people or against our own internal standards for approval).

Self-compassion refers to how warm we can be for ourselves, especially when we're going through a tough time.

People with high self-confidence but low self-esteem and low self-compassion are not uncommon. These people can consider themselves capable, but they don't really like themselves anymore for it, and they can be extremely hard on themselves when they fail.

According to recent behavioural science studies, focusing on self-compassion rather than self-esteem can be better. Self-acceptance underpins the former, while self-evaluation and social contrast underpin the latter. Self-esteem is something like a roller coaster, based on how we think we stack up against others. It also has a strong connection to narcissism.

Individuals who score high on self-compassion scales have more emotional endurance in the face of everyday challenges and have less negative responses to stressful circumstances, such as getting unflattering reviews. Higher self-compassion helps predict levels of accountability by predicting a greater sense of personal responsibility for the outcome of events. Self-compassion is associated with a lower propensity for denial in people. This makes sense: people would be more likely to confess personal errors if they were subjected to less self-criticism.

When people hear the word "self-compassion," they sometimes conjure up images of self-indulgence or self-pity. Surprisingly, this is not the case. The higher the level of self-compassion, the lower one's level of self-pity, according to solid behavioural science studies. The distinction between the two can be thought of as follows: Self-compassion is the feeling that something bad happened to you, while self-pity is the feeling that something bad happened to you, and self-pity is the feeling that something bad happened to you unfairly. Self-pity may lead to anger or bitterness, as well as a sense of isolation and alienation. Self-compassion, on the other hand, often contributes to enhanced feelings of connectedness.

Self-compassion is what allows us to forgive ourselves when we fall short; it's what keeps internal judgment from taking over and ruining our charismatic potential. Self-compassion is important for radiating warmth in this way. Self-compassion, it turns out, will also help you radiate more self-assurance.

Reduced anxiety, depression, and self-criticism; strengthened relationships and feelings of social connectedness and satisfaction with life; increased capacity to manage negative events; and even improved immune system functioning are all advantages of self-compassion.

Doesn't it sound fantastic? Self-compassion isn't taught in schools, unfortunately. In reality, it sounds indulgent and unjustified in today's culture, and it can feel very foreign. To begin with, many of us don't have a very good understanding of what it is.

When things in our lives go wrong, it's tempting to believe that other people have it worse. Rather than feeling lonely and alienated, recognize that someone has or will have the same experience you are having now.

When our critic within starts pointing out our transgressions and flaws, it may make us feel like someone else is doing better than us as if we're the only ones who are this flawed. When our misery appears to be caused by our own perceived shortcomings and inadequacies, self-criticism is far greater than when it appears to be caused by external circumstances. This is the time when self-compassion is most valuable.

What is the best way to cultivate self-compassion? The good news is that the most important aspect of treating yourself with kindness is your purpose. You're able to move on to the more rigorous self-compassion exercises.

USING YOUR BODY TO INFLUENCE YOUR THOUGHTS

So far, we've often spoken about how our mind influences our body—how our mental and emotional states influence our posture, body language, and facial expressions. But did you know that the mechanism can also be reversed? Emotions and body language are so intertwined that adopting a certain pose or facial expression can elicit the same feelings in your head. You can reverse-engineer several emotions by implementing the corresponding body language, just as you can with imagination, where the right picture creates corresponding emotions and body language.

Displaying confident body language will make you feel more confident, which will influence your body language, which will adjust to reflect your emotions, displaying even more confident signals. This will give you a new sense of well-being, and the cycle will continue. All you have to do now is start it. Try out the following postures to see if the way your body is arranged can have a big impact on your mind and emotions.

- To begin, adopt the demeanour of someone who is completely depressed. Allow your shoulders to sag, your head to hang, and your face to droop. Try to get really, really excited without moving a muscle. Go ahead and see if you can elicit some enthusiasm without moving your body. It's almost unlikely.
- Do the polar opposite now. Physically become enthralled. Jump up as if you've won the lottery, smile as wide as you can, wave your arms in the air, and pretend to be sad while doing so. It's almost unlikely once more.

Here are several more physiological shifts to experiment with:

- Imagine yourself in the position of a military general: take a large stance, puff up your chest, spread your shoulders, stand straight, and firmly place your arms behind your back to exude courage, assertiveness, and gravitas. Internally, note how this pose affects you.

- Get up, stretch your hands as far as you can, and inhale as deeply as you can—imagine your rib cage widening and doubling in size.

PREPARING FOR CRITICAL MOMENTS

Assume you've been preparing to run a marathon. You've run some other races, you're in great shape, and you're ready. What would you do if you arrived at the marathon on the day of the race? Would you ever wait until the starting gun goes off before tearing off at full speed? Obviously not. You'd better take extra precautions to warm up properly.

You can achieve the same effect with charisma. Plan a warm-up phase that will allow you to increase to the desired level gradually. Expect to be on top of your game, going from zero to maximum charisma instantly and at will if you want to ensure peak charismatic results. Pure willpower isn't going to get you there. In reality, understanding willpower is critical to getting there. In reality, it's critical to appreciate how finite our regular reserves of willpower are.

Follow this checklist to plan your internal state and boost your charisma while warming up for an important cause.

- In the hours leading up to the case, go through your plan. Consider how you'll be affected by the events and meetings you've scheduled.
- Avoid any unpleasant encounters if at all possible, and instead, seek out interactions that will improve your morale or comfort.
- Make your own music playlist to help you achieve the desired internal condition. You could make one for energy and self-assurance, another for warmth and empathy, and yet another

for peace and serenity. This is a lot of fun in and of itself, and you can keep adding new songs as much as you like.

This is also a perfect replacement for the visualization exercises from the previous chapter for someone who isn't yet familiar with them. If you really want to optimize your charisma ability, you can use it in place of visualizations, or you can schedule a warm-up in addition to visualization.

When you have a series of calls, meetings, or interviews scheduled, whether in a single day or over the course of a week, it's a good idea to order them from least to most important so that you can practice, learn, and progressively improve your ability and trust. Consider yourself an athlete preparing for a test match or a trial run. If you have several letters or e-mails to write on the same topic, you can use this method. Start with the least important e-mails and work your way up to the most important. Your mind will be more practised, and your writing will be more fluid after you've written four or five e-mails.

How do you guarantee that the positive improvements you've made are permanent now that you've learned how to access the right mental state for charisma? This is where charisma preservation comes into play. If you decided to achieve a new level of physical activity, you'd stick to your workout routine and eat a balanced diet. You wouldn't expect to stay in shape if you didn't go to the gym and ate well on a regular basis. Charisma works on the same principle: use all of the techniques you've learned in the previous chapters on a daily basis to remain charismatic.

CHAPTER SIX

DIFFERENT CHARISMA STYLES

There are various charisma models, just as there are various leadership and personality styles.

We'll look at four different types of charisma in this chapter: concentration, visionary, compassion, and authority. We'll look at how each of these is viewed, how to improve it, and when to employ it.

Of course, there are other types of charisma to consider, but these four are the most useful in everyday life, the easiest to reach, and therefore the most useful to research.

FOCUS CHARISMA: CONFIDENCE AND PRESENCE

The sense of presence is the foundation of focus charisma. It gives the impression that you are truly present with them, listening to them and taking in everything they have to say. People who have focus charisma feel heard, listened to, and understood. This type of charisma should not be underestimated; it has a surprising amount of strength. In industry, focus charisma can be extremely beneficial.

What people pay attention to We evaluate attention charisma solely on the basis of temperament. Since we can detect some distracted, inattentive body language, such signals can easily detract from charismatic attention.

FOCUS CHARISMA DEVELOPMENT

Focus charisma necessitates the ability to concentrate and be fully present. A certain amount of patience, as well as good listening skills, are non-negotiable. Improve the ability to be present to develop focus charisma: use the strategies from the previous chapter's "Presence" (get into your toes!). You'll also need the ability to deal with internal distress that detracts from your charm, so techniques like obligation transfer and delving into sensations are worthwhile to learn.

Until you have it: Focus charisma is the simplest type of charisma to obtain, and it can be shockingly efficient, but it has two major drawbacks. The first is that displaying too little power can come across as overly eager, implying low status or even subservience. Later in this book, you'll learn how to boost the amount of trust you exude. A less common risk is displaying too little warmth, which results in excessive attention. Your conversation can start to feel like an interview, or worse, an interrogation, if you become laser-focused. This is where you must strike a balance between concentration and comfort, approval, or sincere appreciation, and the next two chapters will teach you how to do so. Despite the fact that it is mainly focused on appearance, emphasis on charisma is still essential. Despite the fact that it is largely focused on appearance, emphasis on charisma still necessitates a degree of trust and warmth. You can't completely ignore either dimension.

When do you use it? Almost every business situation calls for focus charisma. It's especially useful when you need people to share knowledge and open up. In reality, this charisma style is ideal for management consultants and other professionals such as lawyers, accountants, and financial advisors. In tough circumstances, such as negotiations or defusing aggressive conversations, focus charisma can be extremely beneficial. Focus charisma, on the other hand, should be avoided when you need to appear authoritative or when you need immediate enforcement.

BELIEF AND TRUST IN VISIONARY CHARISMA

Visionary charisma inspires others and makes us believe in ourselves. It can be extremely powerful, even if it does not guarantee that people will like you.

What is it about innovative charisma that makes it so effective and powerful? Since we are naturally averse to confusion. We crave something strong to cling to in a world that is constantly changing. The ability to project full conviction and faith in a cause is required to project visionary charisma. Total belief and trust in a cause can be achieved in this way. Visionary charisma is built on power in this way. It is, however, also dependent on warmth. Visionary charismatics aren't always wet, but they care deeply, even intensely, about what they believe in. Their vision must also contain a certain amount of nobility and altruism to be genuinely charismatic.

What people pay attention to Visionary charisma is judged mainly on the basis of demeanour, which includes body language and actions. People tend to believe whatever you project, so if you seem to be motivated, they'll think you're inspired about something. The presence of visionary charisma is much less important than it is for other charisma types. You may be dressed in rags and yet exude revolutionary charisma.

VISIONARY CHARISMA CREATION

For visionary charisma, the message is crucial. This necessitates the ability to craft a bold vision as well as the charismatic delivery of the message.

One of the most important aspects of expressing revolutionary charisma is to achieve total conviction and eliminate any doubt. You can use the strategies you learned in previous chapters to reinforce your conviction, such as rewriting facts or transferring responsibility, to free yourself from the effects of ambiguity.

Once you've got it, visionary charisma will elicit fervent belief and propel massive change. It can, however, instil fanatical beliefs and lead to catastrophic decisions.

When do you use it? When you need to inspire others, visionary charisma is essential. It's particularly useful for inspiring imagination. Kindness Charisma: Warmth and Confidence

Whatever you do as a kid, your parents will think you're fine just the way you are. However, their approval becomes conditional after a few months. To gain acceptance, you must now eat your carrots and smile. With the exception of the first few stages of falling in love, you will rarely feel such utter unconditional acceptance from someone again.

Warmth is the foundation of kindness charisma. It touches people's souls, making them feel welcomed, loved, embraced, and, most importantly, fully accepted.

What people pay attention to Kindness charisma, like visionary and concentration charisma, is entirely based on body language—specifically, your face, and even more specifically, your eyes.

DEVELOPING A CHARISMA OF KINDNESS

Since the charisma of kindness is highly reliant on warmth, it's critical to avoid any stress, criticism, or coldness in your body language. Internal techniques for coping with mental or physical distress can be extremely useful in this situation.

When you have it, do the following: While warmth is at the heart of kindness charisma, if you lack strength, you risk coming across as too eager to please. This is where the ability to communicate a semblance of authority becomes crucial.

Visualization, warming up and using your body to shift your mind are all strategies that can help you get into the right mindset. The chapters that follow will assist you in balancing warmth and strength in your body language.

When do you use it? When you want to build an emotional connection or make people feel happy and secure, kindness charisma is ideal. In certain cases, such as when you have to share bad news, it can be crucial. When interacting with difficult people, it can also be a surprisingly useful method. However, just as with emphasis charisma, you may want to avoid it if you need to appear authoritative or if you don't want people to feel too comfortable and share too much information.

STATUS AND CONFIDENCE: AUTHORITY CHARISMA

This form of charisma is perhaps the most potent of all. Our natural deference to authority can reach monumental proportions, and it can, of course, be used for good or bad.

THOSE WITH CHARM AND POWER AREN'T ALWAYS LIKEABLE

What people pay attention to Authority charisma is primarily based on a sense of power: the conviction that this individual has the ability to influence the world around them. Body language, voice, title, and other people's reactions are all used to assess someone's authority charisma.

First and foremost, we assess body language. Is there a sense of assurance in the person's ability to impact others or affect the world around them?

Second, we look at how somebody looks. We are biologically conditioned to think for and be impressed by status because it benefits our survival: high-status people have the ability to support or harm us. We must know our place in the pecking order in order to survive. As a result, we're extremely sensitive to any cues that can assist us in determining the status of others.

Clothing is one of our first and most powerful indicators of social status, and therefore future influence and authority charisma. We search for signs of high authority (doctors' white coats) or competence (white coats) (military or police uniforms). We pay special attention to indicators of high social status or achievement, such as expensive clothes.

Finally, a person's title and how others respond to them provide additional information about their authority charisma, but these last two variables are less important than the first two. We instinctively recognize that someone with a high title but no respect has less real influence than someone with a lower title but a lot of respect.

Even though all of these evaluations can take less than a second, the order is crucial. In the event of a signal dispute, we'll trust the signals in the order you just saw. Body language, as always, takes precedence over all other indicators of charisma. Even if all of the other cues are present, insecure body language will derail any attempt at authority charisma. In contrast, if your body language is good enough, you will achieve a certain amount of authority charisma.

INCREASING YOUR AUTHORITY CHARISMA

If you want to achieve authority charisma, the most important thing you can do is project influence by showing signs of status and trust. Fortunately, you have the most control over the two most essential aspects of status and confidence: body language and appearance.

Since body language has such an impact on authority charisma, it is highly influenced by how positive you are at the time. This is where the techniques you learned come in handy: you can use visualizations, warm-ups, or your body to train your mind to think positively.

You'll need to learn how to you Can take up space with your stance, minimize nonverbal reassurances (such as constant nodding), and stop fidgeting to project strength and trust in your body language. It's possible that you'll need to speak less, speak more slowly, know when to pause your sentences, or modulate your intonation. We'll go through what you need to know about projecting power through your body language.

Choosing clothing that tends to be costly or high-status is one of the simplest ways to appear authoritative in terms of appearance.

Once you have it, you will be listened to and always obeyed because of your authority charm. It does, however, have a number of drawbacks:

- It can make you look arrogant;
- It doesn't invite input, so you risk not receiving the information you actually need;
- It can quickly hinder critical thought in others;
- It doesn't invite feedback, so theirs is a high risk of not receiving the information you actually need.

Learning to radiate warmth may be your saving grace in this situation. Your warmth will not only minimize the risk of being seen as arrogant or threatening, but it will also be more highly regarded because you are now seen as a high-status individual. We may find it fun if a low-status individual is eager to satisfy us, but we may not place a high value on their eagerness. After all, they can't do anything for us; it's up to us to help them out. On the other side, we're ecstatic if a high-status alpha gives us attention and comfort because they have the power to lift mountains.

When do you use it? Many business situations, as well as any situation where you want people to listen and comply, benefit from authority charisma. It's especially useful in a crisis or when you need people to obey you right away. However, you can stop it in social circumstances like weddings or funerals, as well as insensitive business situations like delivering bad news. It's also best to avoid it if you want to foster imagination or positive criticism in others, as it can stifle critical thought. Instead, use visionary, concentration, or warmth charisma in these situations.

SELECTING THE APPROPRIATE CHARISMA

There is no one-size-fits-all approach to charisma, and no one charismatic style works in every case. When do these charismatic styles work in all situations? When are some styles more successful than others? Which design is best for you? A critical step toward realizing your charisma ability is determining your favourite charisma style and knowing when to use it.

In various situations, different types of charisma would be sufficient. And various types of charisma will suit you better or worse. To determine which aspects of charisma to emphasize, consider three factors: what is ideally suited to your personality, interests, and circumstance.

- **Personality traits**: It's critical to know what feels good for you and to choose styles, tools, and techniques that complement your unique abilities.
- **The objectives**: You should have a good idea of what you want to accomplish. Some types of charisma will compel people to follow you, while others will encourage them to open up and express their feelings.
- **The situation**: What is the sense into which you are stepping? The circumstance creates the stage for your charm to shine.

YOU'VE GOT THE RIGHT CHARISMA

The first thing to remember is your basic personality. To be charismatic, you don't have to push yourself into one type, and I strongly advise against doing something that goes against your values: it will only work against you. It can be as unpleasant as it is ineffective, and try to push yourself into a charisma style that isn't right for you. An introvert pushing himself to be extroverted, for example, will feel unnatural and awkward, and some may view him as such. He'd not only put himself through a humiliating encounter, but he'd also fail in his attempt to appear naturally extroverted. Rather than battling it, learning how to work in your natural style will pay off big time.

You don't have to push yourself into one charismatic form, and you certainly don't have to limit yourself to just one. In fact, you can switch between many different charismatic modes at any time. You can be more flexible if you learn several modes.

Highly charismatic individuals have the potential to adapt to a wide range of social circumstances. It's really just a matter of gaining access to various facets of your personality and learning to communicate them—we all have a measure of compassion or a modicum of authority within us. Each style will progressively become more normal as you practice it. When you practice these habits enough, they become as natural and relaxed as brushing your teeth.

You can mix and match charisma modes, adding a touch of compassion to your authority charisma or injecting some confident authority into your focus charisma. During a single interview, Oprah can show concentration, compassion, and even revolutionary charisma.

Remember to consider your mental and emotional condition when selecting a charisma style. If you're insecure, wait until you've recovered your trust before attempting to project authority charisma. Instead, opt for a charismatic style that requires less self-assurance, such as concentration or compassion, and then progress to authority if desired. Alternatively, take the time to build your trust so that you can project authority charisma.

The target you want to achieve is the second factor to consider when choosing a charisma type. What do you like people to think about you? What do you want their reaction to being? For example, authority charisma is ideal if you want to be heard and obeyed. The preceding sections gave you an idea of which charisma style is better for achieving which goal. You'll get a sense of which style fits best in various situations when you practice each one.

EACH SITUATION NEEDS A DIFFERENT CHARISMA

The condition you're in is the third factor to consider when choosing a charisma theme. There are numerous circumstances in life where certain types of charisma, no matter how powerful, are undesirable. On the other hand, such cases necessitate complex types of charisma.

The environment in which you work determines how people view you and your charisma.

Let's start with the emotional sense. People's emotional states have an impact on how they perceive you and can either improve or hinder your charisma. People are more likely to find you charismatic while you are in such emotional states, such as a sense of crisis or urgency. However, charisma will exist without a crisis: Before the events of 9/11, President George W. Bush was regarded as charismatic.

Simply ask yourself this question How are the people around you feeling? To get a sense of the emotional background. What do they want right now? If you're firing somebody, authority charisma might not be the best fit; instead, concentration or kindness charisma may be more appropriate. And, like Oprah, you can switch between multiple types of charisma, relying on various facets of your personality as you adapt to different situations.

It's also important to consider the social context: one action can be charismatic in the United States but not in Japan. In parts of Asia, the same amount of eye contact that is welcomed as an honest, direct look in most of North America can be perceived as offensive and obnoxious. Though the fundamental elements of charisma are presence, warmth, and strength, how they are expressed differs from culture to culture.

Having said that, if you set your mind and behaviour right, you'll be 80 per cent of the way there. Since facial expressions are common, a gesture of goodwill, empathy, or concern in New York will be viewed the same way in China or even France.

More importantly, people place a high value on the motives you seem to have. So, if you can get yourself into a mental state of goodwill, it will manifest in your facial expressions and body language, and it will register with people on a deep emotional level. People who see this would want to like you and see your acts and attitudes in the best light possible. Consider goodwill to be your charisma safety net: if you can maintain a positive attitude, you'll have the greatest chance of nailing your charisma (you can refer back for goodwill-boosting techniques).

CHAPTER SEVEN

CHARISMATIC FIRST IMPRESSIONS

You don't get another chance to make a good first impression. People have judged your social and economic status, level of education, and even level of achievement in a matter of seconds and with only a glance. They've even agreed on your intellect, trustworthiness, integrity, friendliness, and confidence levels in minutes. While these assessments are made in a split second, they may last for years: first impressions are always permanent.

Is it possible to recover from an unfavourable first impression? Yes, that is right. You may sometimes alter a person's initial impression of you over the course of many meetings. However, you'll have to put in a lot more effort than if you come across as charismatic right away.

WHY DO SECOND-BY-SECOND SENSATIONS LAST SO LONG?

If you make a good first impression on another, it will colour the rest of your relationship, thus tipping the scales in your favour. An adverse first impression, on the other hand, can be difficult to resolve, frequently determining the outcome of a meeting even though the rest of the interaction is flawless. Litigators understand how important a client's first impression on a jury can be in determining the outcome of a case, and they, therefore, spend hours training them for it. This is why, even though you're running late for a meeting, it's worth investing thirty seconds to re-establish the proper mental and physical condition. Otherwise, you run the risk of making an unappealing first impression.

Another explanation first impressions have such power is that they are always right.

"We've known for a long time that people make snap judgments about others based on very little information," one of the researchers said, "but what's surprising about these results is how many of the impressions have a kernel of truth to them, also based on a single photograph."

Further research has shown that we are always very accurate in our assessments of personality, even after just a few seconds of meeting someone.

If there's a possibility the individual is an adversary, the next question is whether to fight or flee. Will they be able to carry out their nefarious plans if they had the ability to do so? Our brain tries to figure out who will prevail in a battle to find the answer. We take into account things like height and weight, age, and gender.

The substance of what we say and how we say it comes into play only after all of these tests have taken place.

THE GOLDEN RULE IS A SET OF GUIDELINES THAT SHOULD BE FOLLOWED

So, what would you do to make a great first impression? The default setting is actually very straightforward: people prefer people who are similar to them. People lived in tribes for the vast majority of our history, which is where our present instincts come from. In such a situation, being able to tell whether or not someone belongs to your tribe may mean the difference between life and death. You've already won half the fight if you can get these instinctive reactions to work in your favour.

When people's dress, appearance, personality, and expression are identical, they immediately presume they have similar social backgrounds, education, and values.

Before posture and body language, the overall appearance is assessed. This may be due to the fact that clothing can be seen from a greater distance, allowing us to decide more easily whether the other individual is a friend or foe, a fellow tribesman or not. Clothing is basically contemporary tribal wear.

TRIBAL APPAREL

Clothing matters, no matter how objective we try to be. When delivered in a suit versus a nightgown, the same speech would be interpreted quite differently.

Look at the variety of options inside that setting and select the upper end if you want to impress others. There's a reason for the expression "dress to impress."

It's worthwhile to do your homework. If you're going to a wedding, call the host; if you're going to a work interview, stop by the office a few days ahead of time to see what people are wearing when they come in and out.

THE IMPORTANCE OF A FIRM HANDSHAKE

Your first impression will suffer no matter how costly your suit, watch, or briefcase is if your handshake is bad. A good handshake is far less expensive and can do far more for you than a designer suit. A strong handshake is essential for authority charisma—imagine a dominant figure with a shaky, limp handshake.

A handshake, while seemingly insignificant, is a significant move toward intimacy. The physical contact necessitates the suspension of the personal space barrier, even if only for a brief moment. As a result, confidence is required. The first step in a relationship is taken if the confidence is established (the handshake goes well).

Shaking the right hand, which was historically used to wield weapons, was indicative of a suspension of threat, indicating that the greeter's weapon hand was unarmed.

Let's look at the worst of the many handshake blunders that people can create.

The Dead Fish: This is, without a doubt, the worst. A lifeless, limp hand is stretched and barely shaken here. This lifeless handshake is extended and only shaken.

The Dominant: This grip could be a display of machismo, but it may also be the product of someone who is genuinely unsure of his (or her) power. It may also be the product of erroneous teachings, such as the belief that the tighter a woman's grasp, the more seriously she would be taken. As a result, they come to the conclusion that they should tighten up as if their lives depended on it.

The Knuckle Cruncher: The hand is extended palm down in this situation, possibly indicating the desire to get the upper hand in the relationship. The Twisting Dominant is a variant of this shake in which the hand is innocently stretched straight outward but bends once the shake is initiated to obtain the upper hand.

The Double-Handed: The classic two-handed handshake will bring this dreadful list to a close. Your partner's left hand will be at work in this situation, closing in on your right hand, shoulder, wrist, arm or neck. It's also referred to as The Politician's Handshake, which shows how little respect people have for those who give it.

So, what are the components of a flawless handshake? The ten components of a gold-star handshake can be found in the list below.

1. First and foremost, ensure that your right hand is free. Shift everything it's holding to your left hand as soon as possible. You don't want to be scrambling at the last minute.

2. Keeping a drink in your right hand, particularly if it's a cold drink, will make your hand feel cold and clammy due to condensation.

3. If you're sitting, rise before shaking someone's hand, whether you're a man or a woman. Also, keep your hands out of your pockets: they seem more transparent and genuine when they are visible. Be sure to make eye contact and smile a lot.

4. Maintain strong eye contact and smile warmly but briefly; too much smiling can make you look agitated.

5. Keep your head straight and completely face the guy without leaning in any direction.

6. Maintain complete perpendicularity with your side, neither dominant (palm down) nor submissive (palm up) (palm up). When in doubt, point your thumb straight up at the ceiling.

7. To ensure optimum thumb-web touch, widen the distance between your thumb and index finger.

8. Maintain a palm-to-palm touch by holding your palm flat (not cupped) and draping your hand diagonally over your partner's.

9. Curl your fingers around your partner's palm, one by one, as if you were hugging them. You'll almost be able to feel their pulse with your index finger—almost, but not yet.

If you've made full contact, lock your thumb down and grip as hard as your partner. Shake from the elbow (not the wrist), stay for a moment if you want to express specific warmth, and then step back.

So you've already made a great first impression. You have a fantastic handshake. What happens when you approach them? You are the one who speaks. Conversationalists with charisma know how to quickly start a conversation, make people feel unique, and finish it gracefully. Let's look at how you can build meaningful connections from beginning to end, from how you start a conversation to how you end it.

LET'S BREAK THE ICE

Offering a compliment about what the individual is wearing is a simple way to start conversations in a way that both expresses warmth and leads the conversation in the right direction. This would be an excellent opener if you were to project either kindness or emphasis charisma. If you know a more subdued version of your authority charisma is required, it can also be a good way to balance out the strength in your authority charisma.

Continue with an open-ended question like, "What's the backstory?" The word "plot" has a powerful emotional impact on most people, causing them to go into storytelling mode, altering your relationship immediately. Furthermore, they are most definitely optimistic about this item because they want to wear it.

"Where are you from?" is another good icebreaker issue. Whatever the response is, it will elicit further discussion.

Simply ask open-ended questions like, "What brought you here tonight?" or "How are you related to this event?" to keep people talking. Closed questions, on the other hand, can only be answered with yes or no, and once answered, you're back where you started, trying to come up with something new to keep the conversation going.

Keep your questions optimistic in nature so people can connect you with the emotions that your conversation evokes. You'd probably instinctively know not to ask, "So, how's the divorce going?" Rather, concentrate on issues that are likely to evoke optimistic feelings. You have the ability to steer the conversation in the direction you want with your questions.

They are using the bounce-back tactic if they start talking about you and you want to refocus the conversation on them. Use the bounce-back technique to react to their conversation. Respond to the question with a fact, a personal note, and redirection to them.

Bear in mind that the aim is to keep the spotlight on them for as long as possible. And when chatting, the one word that should come up most often in your conversation is you, not I.

Adapt your word use, vocabulary breadth and scope, and phrases to fit your audience: concentrate on their areas of interest and use metaphors from those domains to make yourself more relatable. Suppose you're talking about success with someone who enjoys golf, mention finding a hole in one. A disaster becomes a shipwreck if they sail.

EXITING IN STYLE

The last few moments, like the first impression, will colour the rest of the interaction. People would enjoy being around you if you become a charismatic conversationalist, and they will be reluctant to let you go. Indeed, the more charming you become, the more difficult it will be to avoid your newfound admirers. This is mentioned by many charismatic people as one of their greatest challenges. So, how can you end a discussion gracefully?

To begin, don't wait too long to put an end to it. Otherwise, both you and your partner will feel strained and uneasy. Having an official excuse to leave is, of course, the simplest way to do so. One of the many reasons to volunteer or take on an official position at a party is to help others. People would expect you to spend no more than a few minutes with them while you're "on duty."

Offering value to others will always elicit feelings of warmth and gratitude from them, and your exit from the discussion will be accompanied by the impression of kindness you've made.

Wait until the person you are having the conversation with has finished a sentence before saying something like, "You know, based on what you just said, you should really check out this Web site." If the individual has decided to meet everyone in the room, simply say, "Let me introduce you," and they will be brought together. Your discussion partner can't help but feel good about you because you've just given them something generously. You may also bring others into the discussion as they walk by—often, it's easier to leave a party of three or four.

What if you're the one who separates a group? Perhaps you're saving anyone from a discussion they've suggested they'd like to quit, maybe you need to introduce them to someone else, or one of the group members is required to perform another task.

In this situation, concentrate all of your attention, with especially warm eye contact, on the person who is being left behind, rather than the person you're taking with you. This reduces the likelihood of them feeling excluded, and it's especially crucial when expressing either kindness or emphasis on charisma.

You may not recall the exact content of conversations from a week ago, but you are likely to recall how they made you feel. The emotional imprint of the conversation, not the words, is what remains. And if you use any of the resources we've just talked about, the emotional impact will be incredible.

CHAPTER EIGHT

SPEAKING AND LISTENING WITH CHARISMA

As we've seen, nonverbal gestures such as body language and facial expressions can send a number of messages and can be used to project charisma even before a single word is spoken. The first move is to cultivate a charismatic mental state, but this chapter will reveal unique verbal and vocal strategies for effectively broadcasting your charismatic mental state. When listening, you'll learn how to communicate presence, and when speaking, you'll learn how to communicate strength and warmth.

LISTENING TO THAT IS CHARISMATIC

You can make people feel fully heard and understood without saying something by being a great listener. In reality, impressing people solely through words is surprisingly easy. It's actually surprisingly simple to impress people simply by paying attention.

We're about to go through three important aspects of expressing presence: attentive listening, refraining from interrupting, and deliberate pausing. Listening comes first since it establishes the foundation for the appearance that is essential to charisma.

I'm sure you understand the importance of listening. But did you know that with only a few modifications, your listening skills can go from decent to exceptional? The desire and mental capacity to be present, pay attention, and reflect on what the other person is saying are the foundations of good listening skills. As you would expect, this is critical for conveying emphasis on charisma, but it can also help with other charisma types.

One of the most popular blunders is equating listening with "allowing others to speak before it's my turn." Sorry, but that isn't enough. You can't let your mind be elsewhere while waiting for your turn to chat, even though the other person is doing all the talking. Your lack of presence will be all over your face, even though what you're worried about is what you want to say next. The other person will notice you aren't completely present and are simply waiting for them to finish before jumping in.

Effective listening requires a high level of presence. You already have everything you need to keep your mind from wandering as someone else speaks:

• If zoning out is a problem, concentrate on physical sensations like the vibration in your toes or the movement of your breath in and out of your body; if impatience is a problem, address it by delving into the minute physical sensations you're experiencing. Then return to the person.

How do you ensure the right habits if you have the right mindset? Effective listening entails acting in such a way that the person with whom you're conversing feels fully understood.

Good listeners know not to interrupt, even though they feel compelled to do so because they are interested in what the other person has just said. No matter how congratulatory and friendly the words are, they will still feel a twinge of disappointment or anger at not being able to finish their sentence.

Great listeners are aware of the importance of allowing others to disturb them. Allow others to disturb you if they so choose. Was it enough for them to interrupt you? Obviously not. But even if they were right, is it worth your time? Obviously not. Even if they were mistaken, it's not worth it to make them feel bad; your job is to make them feel good. Keep your sentences short and leave frequent pauses for the other person to step in if you hear them agitating to talk.

People adore listening to themselves talk. They will like you more if you allow them to talk.

Master listeners have one more trick up their sleeves, a basic but highly successful habit that makes people feel genuinely heard and understood: they pause before responding.

In business discussions, knowing when and how to pause is also an art and something that most charismatic conversationalists do naturally. Pausing, which is an important negotiating technique, can also help people feel good about themselves while they're around you— it's a simple way to make people feel knowledgeable, interesting, and even impressive.

When someone speaks, see if you can let your facial expression respond first, indicating that you're taking in what they've just said and giving their clever comment the attention it deserves. After about two seconds, you finally react. The following is the sequence:

- They finish their sentence
- Your face absorbs
- Your facial response
- Only then can you respond.

Now, I'm not implying that this is a simple task. It takes courage to endure silence, both because of the discomfort you might feel and because you don't know what they're thinking during those two seconds. It is, however, worthwhile.

Great listening skills will improve every charisma style and offer you present, which is the cornerstone of charisma. Let's move on to how you can communicate charismatic warmth and strength now that you've established a strong base for communicating presence.

SPEAKING IN A CHARISMATIC MANNER

Our minds make connections between the sensations we're having and the places, objects, and physical sensations we encounter while we have them. This is why automotive companies often use highly desirable female models in their advertisements.

Others would connect you with the way you make them feel because we associate feelings with sights, sounds, tastes, smells, places, and, of course, people. Making people feel good about themselves is important for most charisma, but particularly kindness charisma.

Since we're constantly making connections in people's minds, it's important to be mindful of how you're making them feel in both business and social contexts. You must build clear positive associations while avoiding negative ones to be charismatic.

USE THIS METHOD TO GAIN ACCEPTANCE AND PRAISE

Accept a Gratitude

Without even noticing it, we sometimes stifle our warmth with negative comparisons. Negative associations can occur if someone feels bad in our presence, but they are especially dangerous if we make people feel bad about themselves— wrong, inadequate, or dumb.

When anyone compliments you, how do you react? Do you instinctively downplay compliments that you look good or that you have done something remarkable, for example? Compliments are both fun and unpleasant for many people, so why not downplay them? Many people find compliments to be both fun and uncomfortable, and they are unsure how to handle them. Many of us either become embarrassed or modestly deflect the praise with phrases like "Oh, it's nothing..."

Unfortunately, this gives the message to your admirer that they complimented you incorrectly. They'll most likely feel stupid, and there's a possibility they'll associate that feeling with you. If you do this often enough, they'll eventually give up. If you make them feel good for complimenting you, on the other hand, they'll enjoy feeling good about themselves and want to do it again.

The following measures will assist you in handling a compliment the next time you receive one:

1. Come to a halt.
2. Take in the compliment with both hands. If you can, take advantage of it.
3. Allow the split second of concentration to reflect on your face. Demonstrate to the individual that they've made a difference.
4. Express gratitude to them. It's enough to say "thank you so much," but you can go a step further by thanking them for their thoughtfulness or telling them how much they've brightened your day.

Making positive comparisons to emphasize the warmth factor means making others feel comfortable when they're around you. What are you going to do to make people feel this way?

First, consider how you would act if you were dealing with the most powerful person in the room. You'd actually be interested in hearing what they had to say. You'd be genuinely curious, maybe even fascinated, and it's that mindset that will make people feel good about themselves and associate those feelings with you.

People who are charismatic are experts at creating positive connections, whether consciously or subconsciously, and you'll always hear people raving about how "special" and "wonderful" they felt after meeting them.

Make no attempt to please anyone. Allow them to impress you, and they will thank you. You don't have to sound intelligent, believe it or not. All you have to do now is make them feel smart.

GET A VISUAL

Indeed, an image is worth a thousand words—and for good purpose. Image production has a significant influence on emotions and physiological states, as well as brain activity. Language processing skills in the brain are much younger and less heavily wired than visual processing abilities. Our visual-processing capacities are harmed because we are heavily wired. When you speak in words, the brain must first connect the words to meanings, then translate those concepts into images, which is how you are understood. Why not talk explicitly to the brain in its native tongue? Choose to talk in pictures whenever possible. You'll make a much bigger impression, and your message will stick with people much longer. The influence of images is fully used by visionary charismatics.

Try to make the pictures and metaphors sensory-rich by using as much of the five senses as possible. You can do this in almost any case, even with the driest of subjects, believe it or not.

Of course, you'll want to use the best metaphor for your specific target with great care. We wanted to shock people and scare them into recalling something important in the previous example. I felt perfectly at ease suggesting a particularly unpleasant metaphor. Consider the emotional tone of your metaphor and make your choices accordingly.

DELIVER HIGH-VALUE SERVICES

Attention, like time and money, is a limited resource. You're asking people to spend both their time and their energy on you when you ask them to listen to what you say or read what you've written. You're requesting that they share some of their resources with you.

In exchange, what are you offering them? You can bet that if people are asked to spend any of their limited money, they are (at least subconsciously) calculating the return on their investment. You may provide value to others in a variety of ways:

- Make your e-mail or meeting more entertaining.
- Information: Provide them with useful or interesting material.
- Positive emotions: Find ways to make them feel important or confident.

The higher the price you make them pay, the more you chat, then the higher the value should be. When rehearsing a new presentation, professional speakers will often have their first attempt taped and transcribed and then go through each sentence with the aim of tightening their speech as much as possible.

In reality, trying to provide high value for little effort brings together all of the points we've discussed so far. Use few words and lots of pictures while speaking or writing, and try to make your interactions informative, fun, and even entertaining.

GETTING YOUR VOICE IN SHAPE

The basis for both vocal warmth and strength is voice fluctuation. Studies have consistently shown that the delivery style of a lecture has a greater impact on audience ratings than the material. Your voice is essential for conveying both warmth and strength, but there is no single charismatic voice. You can wield influence, but there isn't a single charismatic voice. Depending on what you want to say and who you're talking to, you can emphasize various aspects of your speech.

We looked at how to combine speaking and listening earlier in this chapter. Variation is the second essential vocal characteristic. Your persuasiveness and charisma are influenced by how much your voice changes. Increasing voice fluctuation means changing the pitch (high or low), volume (loud or quiet), sound (resonant or hollow), tempo (fast or slow), or rhythm of your voice (fluid or staccato).

VOCAL STRENGTH

Set the pitch of your voice, tone of your voice, the volume of your voice, and tempo of your voice in the following ways if you want to convey power:

Tone and pitch: Your voice would have more effect if it is lower, more resonant, and baritone.

Dimensions: One of the first things a stage actor learns is how to project his voice, which entails learning to modulate its pitch and direct it in such a way that particular parts of the audience can hear it even from afar. Imagine that your words are arrows as a classic exercise to improve your projection skills. Aim them at various groups of listeners as you talk.

Trust is conveyed by a steady, measured tempo with frequent pauses.

WARMTH IN THE VOICE

There's only one thing you needed to make your voice sound warmer: smile. Smiling has such an impact on how we talk that listeners in one study were able to distinguish sixteen different types of smiles just by hearing them. This is why it's important to smile even when you're on the phone.

What about situations where you don't feel compelled to smile? The good news is that you don't have to smile to warm up your voice: sometimes just thinking about smiling is enough. While there is no one-size-fits-all approach to delivering charisma, here is a successful visual that conveys both power and warmth. Assume you're a preacher addressing the flock. Consider a preacher's rich, rolling, resonant voice: he cares for his people (warmth), and he also believes he has the might of God behind him (power, authority, confidence).

Let's look at body language now that you have the resources to express presence, warmth, and power by speaking and listening.

CHAPTER NINE
CHARISMATIC BODY LANGUAGE

Words are first grasped by people's cognitive minds, or rational sides, which set about deciphering their meaning. Body language, on the other hand, has a visceral and emotional effect on us. You must tap into this emotional level in order to encourage others to join, care about, or obey you.

Charisma appeals to our emotional side by impressing, inspiring, or thrillingly unique us. It works in a way that bypasses our rational thought. The emotion of awe, like charisma, goes beyond our comprehension and reaches us on an emotional level.

Nonverbal means of communication are far more deeply ingrained in our brains than more recent language-processing skills, and they have a much greater impact on us. The nonverbal amplifies the verbal when our verbal and nonverbal signals are in sync (when they "agree" with each other). We prefer to trust the nonverbal over the verbal when they are in dispute. It doesn't matter how good your message is if your body language is anti-charismatic. On the other hand, even though the message is flawed, you will succeed with the right body language.

In certain cases, the manner in which a message is delivered has a much greater effect than the message itself. In high-stakes circumstances, such as trying to attract a new client, impress a new boss, or make a new friend, our propensity to respond to how something is said rather than what is said is especially intense.

Since our fight-or-flight response triggers and a more primitive part of the brain takes over in high-stakes situations, we respond more strongly to body language than to words. This portion of the brain does not understand words or thoughts explicitly. Body language, on the other hand, has an immediate influence.

CONTAGION OF EMOTIONS

Because of the phenomenon known as emotional contagion, your body language is especially relevant if you're in a position of leadership. This is described by behavioural scientists as "the mechanism by which one individual's emotions are 'caught' by another." People who are charismatic are said to be more "contagious," meaning they have a great capacity to communicate their feelings to others. Even in small, casual encounters, the emotions reflected by your body language as a leader can have a ripple effect across your team or even your entire organization.

This ripple effect is caused by mirror neurons in our brain, which is responsible for replicating or mirroring in our own minds the feelings we see in others. Our mirror neurons replicate other people's emotions when we sense them through their gestures or facial expressions. Empathy is only possible because of this.

Let's pretend you're having a conversation with someone while feeling nervous. Their mirror neurons light up as they read your body language, mirroring your condition. They go on to find someone else, and the process repeats itself, spreading your emotional state. Emotional contagion kickstart arousal in others in a chain reaction, according to a report. Since people are deeply influenced by those in positions of influence, leaders' emotions often spread the fastest within organizations. Emotional contagion can have a significant impact on the success of your followers.

Emotional contagion can be a wonderful thing when it's optimistic. Leaders' positive emotional contagion has been shown in controlled experimental settings to increase not only their followers' moods, efficiency, and effectiveness but also their followers' perceptions of the leaders' effectiveness.

Emotional contagion will, of course, have a negative impact, so it's worth improving your knowledge of your own internal states, as well as your ability to control your emotions, in order to control the repercussions of this spread. One strong indicator of your charm is the strength of your emotional contagion.

MIRRORING WITH INTENTION

Have you ever noticed how people who have been married for a long time seem to resemble one another? It's a well-known fact that as we spend more time together, we learn to read each other's body language. This naturally involves our facial expressions, which form our faces in similar ways by using the same facial muscles over and over.

This propensity to imitate other people's body language is known as limbic resonance, and it's hardwired into the human brain. Limbic resonance is made possible by oscillators, a type of neuron that coordinates people physically by controlling how and when their bodies move together.

Imitating someone's body language is a simple way to build rapport and trust. This technique, also known as mirroring or mimicking, is the deliberate implementation of something that many charismatic people do without thinking.

When you actively mimic someone's body language, you activate deep confidence and liking instincts. As a result, it can be extremely useful when you need people to open up.

Several studies have shown that mirroring someone's body language will persuade them to pick up your dropped products, purchase your goods, or give you a better price. Mirroring will also increase your attractiveness to others.

Try to imitate the other person's overall stance over the next few conversations: how they keep their head, how they position their feet, and how their weight changes. Shift the right hand if they move their left. Aim to match your voice's rhythm, pitch, and intonation to theirs.

Since people's primary focus while communicating is on themselves, they're unlikely to know you're mirroring unless you make it quite clear. However, there are a few things you can do to improve subtlety:

• **Be selective in your actions**: just do what comes naturally to you. Some gestures, for example, are gender-specific.

• **Vary the amplitude of the gestures**: if they make a large gesture, make a smaller one.

• **Use lag time**: switch into a mirrored location after a few seconds have passed.

But what about when the other person is displaying offensive body language? Do you even use a mirror? Ok, that is debatable. In certain cases, it's best to mimic their body language at first, then gradually shift it to a more constructive direction. Gradually direct in a more positive way.

Let's say one of your coworkers comes in to see you, visibly agitated about something. She timidly taps on your open door, asking for permission to come in. Her movements are tentative as she enters.

When you ask her to tell you what's going on, she seems agitated and drawn inward, as if she can't find the words to articulate her concerns.

Mirroring can be helpful in building rapport in this situation. In this case, you should carefully study her posture—the way she sits, how she holds her head, and how her shoulders are—and progressively adopt the same posture. Look for patterns. Is she occasionally shaking her head? Knocking on her knee? Do you find yourself fidgeting with a button? You may be able to find a way to mirror that as well roughly. Match your voice to hers by adopting a similar cadence, tempo, and volume.

Spend all of your listening time in that mode until you're in a mirrored position: adapt your body language to hers for as long as you're listening. Only when it's your turn to talk can you begin to use your speech, face, and eyes to infuse the conversation with love, empathy, and compassion. As you talk, gradually change your stance to one that is more relaxed, calm, and optimistic.

When the person you're engaging with needs reassurance—when they're nervous or timid, anxious or uncomfortable, rigid or withdrawn—mirror-then-lead is a good technique. Mirror all of these emotional states to build comfort and rapport and then draw them out gradually. It's not good when you try to sway their body language too aggressively in these cases.

On the other hand, there are times when it is inappropriate to imitate someone's body language. Mirroring their demeanour if they are upset or defensive would just add to the tension. Assume you're facing someone who has flatly refused your invitation and is sitting in a defensive posture, arms and legs crossed, and hands balled into fists. Rather than mirroring, try giving him something to break him out of his posture: a piece of paper or a pen—whatever works. Then, as soon as he or she is in a new role, divert their attention by providing new details or changing the topic, all while mirroring his pose to reestablish rapport.

Remember that our psychology is influenced by our physiology. Because of this connection between physiology and psychology, it's critical to get someone who is frustrated, stubborn, or defensive to alter their body language before attempting to change their mind. It would be almost impossible to get their mind to feel something else as long as their body is in a certain emotional mode.

PERSONAL SPACE

Depending on which stalls are already filled, people consistently follow a particular pattern. Our personal room is still occupied due to our adherence to personal space law. Our adherence to concerning personal space rules is so high that people who play virtual reality games have been found to follow real-life personal space rules when playing the game.

The idea of personal space arose from observations of zoo animals' behaviour in the mid-twentieth century. We humans experience "ownership" of the environment around us in the same way as animals identify and protect their territories. Even if it's just a few centimetres, this territory feels like an extension of our bodies, and we act to protect it and retaliate forcefully if it's violated.

When others are around us, being charismatic means making them feel at ease, relaxed, and good about themselves. Respecting the level of personal space people need to be relaxed is an important aspect of nonverbal communication for making people feel at ease and building rapport. Respecting people's personal space expectations, on the other hand, may cause a lot of discomforts, and those feelings can come to be associated with you. It's worthwhile to pay attention.

Let's say you're having a conversation with someone, and you find that she's leaning away from you with her upper body, pulling her head backwards, or even physically moving away from you. This may indicate that she needs more personal space. Moving in closer would be the worst thing you could do. That would exacerbate her frustration, and there's a fair chance she'd associate those feelings with you. Instead, give her some breathing room by leaning away or moving back a few inches.

Personal space varies according to culture, population density, and circumstance. The comfort zone of a single person is extremely variable. We are willing to consider personal space limitations that are, in fact, very variable. In such cases, such as a packed elevator, bus, or subway, we can embrace personal space constraints.

Our relationships with others and how we view circumstances are influenced by our personal space. That is, for example, why negotiators select their seats at a table with such care; they understand that their seating choice will affect the outcome of the entire negotiation. When people are seated across from each other with a table separating them, they talk in shorter sentences, are more likely to disagree, and have a harder time remembering what was said.

Avoid seating anyone with their back to open space if you want them to feel at ease, particularly if others are moving behind them. This type of seating position causes rapid increases in breathing rate, heart rate, and blood pressure, particularly if the person's back is against an open door or a window at ground level. And, as a result, their dissatisfaction would most likely influence how they perceive you.

THE WINDOWS TO YOUR SOUL ARE YOUR EYES

Have you ever had n a conversation with someone who kept looking behind you to see if someone more important or interesting was approaching? Those wandering eyes aren't exactly charismatic.

It's crucial to maintain good eye contact. Deep eye contact has a powerful effect on people; it can express empathy as well as convey thoughtfulness, insight, and intellect. It's impossible to be charismatic without it. In reality, one of the key ways charismatic masters make you feel like you're the most important person in the room is through eye contact.

Our eyes are probably the single most significant aspect of our nonverbal communication. Why are the eyes referred to as the "windows to the soul"? They're the most expressive because they're the most mobile part of the face.

Assume you're having a conversation with a person who is wearing sunglasses. Wouldn't it be more difficult to decipher them?

Eye contact is so important to us that when someone with whom we have significant eye contact turns away, our brains are hardwired to feel separation distress. Maintaining eye contact for three full seconds at the end of your interaction with others is a safe way to stop causing anxiety. This will appear to be short, but it will feel endless! You'll find it well worth the effort if you can get into the habit of doing so. People would believe you have actually paid attention to them after only a few seconds of investment.

Lack of eye contact, which is mainly caused by shyness and lack of eye contact due to distraction are two of the most common eye contact problems. Unfortunately, either of these factors will derail your charismatic ability. Delving into sensations is a technique that works equally well with all of these. Pay attention to the physical feelings you are experiencing when you gaze into someone's eyes. If shyness is a problem, this will help to de-emphasize the situation. If shyness is an issue, this will help to de-emphasize the situation. This strategy will help you keep your mind centred in the present moment if the distraction is a problem. You may also examine the various colours in their eyes, as well as the various shades that play around their pupils.

These tips and tools will assist you in making the appropriate amount of eye contact. But that's not enough—you really need to know how to make the right kind of eye contact to be charismatic. The amount and type of stress we display around our eyes have a significant effect on how we are viewed.

Switching to a softer emphasis is needed for charismatic eye contact. This automatically calms our stress system and relaxes our eyes and face. To help you transition to a soft, open focus, follow these three easy steps: Close your eyes first. Focus your attention on the space with a light, open focus: Close your eyes first. Concentrate on the empty space in the room and the space around you. Now concentrate on the vast expanse of space that encompasses the entire universe. That's it—you've entered "soft focus."

You were right when you said that eye contact was essential. Few things detract from charisma more than poor eye contact, and few things increase charisma more than enhancing it. Try to keep an eye on whether your eyes are stressed the next time you're in a discussion. If you notice even a smidgeon of tension around your eyes, try to calm them. To switch into soft focus, you can use any favourite fast visualization or goal.

It's crucial to get your eyes in the right place if you want to radiate warmth. Let's take a look at one of the most important aspects of power: posture.

THE CORRECT POSTURE FOR NONVERBAL INFLUENCE

Since we can't see into people's hearts and minds, we make assumptions based on what we see. When we see someone with a lot of pride in their body language, we think they have something to be positive about: people just believe what you project. Any boost in the amount of trust you project through your body language would pay off handsomely in terms of charisma.

You will exude warmth, enthusiasm, and excitement without coming across as too eager or subservient if you project power and trust. Since body language is so profoundly ingrained in us, signs of trust (or lack thereof) in someone's body language trump all other signs of strength. A body language of vulnerability can destroy charisma on the spot, no matter how many signs of power and high status we may project through our appearance, title, or even others' deference. A confident body language, on the other hand, will endow the bearer with charisma even if no other power signs are present.

In the parts that follow, you'll learn how to project strength in your stance and poise while maintaining a sense of warmth.

ROYALTY STANCE

The lack of movement that characterizes this type of high-status, high-confidence body language is notable. People who are composed have a calmness about them that is often referred to as poise. They avoid making unnecessary movements like fidgeting with their clothing, hair, or faces, shaking their heads incessantly, or saying "um" before sentences.

These movements, which behaviour experts classify as low-status, are often used by people who want to reassure the individual with whom they're communicating. The need to reassure others may come from two different places:

• **Insecurity**: trying to satisfy or appease the person you're engaging with

• **Empathy**: wanting to make sure the other person feels noticed and understood and that you're paying attention

People who come across as strong, confident, or high-status, on the other hand, are generally more restrained; they don't feel the need to reassure because they aren't as concerned with what their counterpart is thinking.

There are three big problems to watch out for if you want to improve your poise. The first is quick or excessive nodding. Nodding once for emphasis or to convey approval is acceptable and can be a useful communication tool, but nodding three or four times in a row is not.

Excessive verbal reassurance is the second barrier: making a sound, such as "uh-huh," or a half-sentence, such as "Oh, I agree." This is perfect if done once and consciously; several times per sentence is not.

The third problem is fidgeting or restlessness. Fidgeting reduces the presence and, as a result, charisma. You can't be charismatic if you're physically restless, even if you're wet, confident, and mentally present. Distracting messages are being sent by your body language.

How can you get rid of these bad habits? The first step is to become conscious of how you look to others. You can videotape yourself during a meeting or even a casual conversation, which is one of the most important things you can do. Quick forward ten minutes from the time you sit down to watch it; you'll have forgotten about the camera long enough to show uninhibited body language. Start by turning off the sound and observing the body language (nodding, gesturing, etc.) in comparison to the most senior person in the room. Then, with the sound on, watch it again and compare your level of verbal reassurance to others'. Though the experience can be frustrating, it's also beneficial: you'll know that what you see on the tape is also what others see. You should be conscious of it as well.

With this newfound understanding, you can notice yourself showing a lot of verbal and nonverbal reassurance during the day and be surprised by how often it happens. This is perfectly natural.

Allow yourself to relax. This cycle of anger affects all, and it is possible to break these patterns.

However, keep in mind that exuding too much power might come across as arrogant or threatening to some people. This will be countered by the warmth-enhancing strategies you learned earlier in this chapter, such as keeping your eyes in soft focus. Imagine a president bowing his head to a noble emissary by bringing the chin down a few degrees. This has two advantages. It prevents you from appearing contemptuously staring down your nose at others (as is the case when your head is turned back) while also making you appear more reflective, attentive, and deliberate as your eyes naturally open wider.

Knowing What to Do in Different Situations

In one situation, the same amount of nonverbal contact or reassurance may be necessary and beneficial, but in another, it may be counterproductive. For example, if you want to make a nervous colleague or subordinate feel at ease and open up, you should use both (nodding) and verbal (uh-huh) reassurance in your interactions.

If they seem nervous and you believe they need reassurance, increase the amount of warmth you project. Use some of the warmth-enhancing visualizations or verbal warmth strategies you learned in class, and match your body language to theirs.

When you want to be seen as a confident peer or a valued boss, on the other hand, concentrate on poise and containment while limiting your reassurance. Stick to your own rhythms and preserve your positive, contained stance rather than synchronizing your body language with theirs (unless theirs is the very essence of trust you want to display).

You now know how to use both verbal and nonverbal communication to project presence, strength, and warmth.

You learned how to create a strong internal base for charisma before moving on to how to carry your charisma out into the world. You're now able to learn how to use these techniques in challenging circumstances. The following chapter will show you how to maintain your charm when it matters most.

CHAPTER TEN

DIFFICULT SITUATIONS

However, as you would expect, some difficult situations might necessitate a more complex approach. You'll learn how to deal with challenging people, deliver bad news or criticism, and make apologies in the most charismatic way possible in this chapter. It is possible to emerge from both of these encounters with your relationships intact, if not improved.

MANAGING DIFFICULT PEOPLE

Some people are simply impossible to deal with. Some people need their egos stroked, others are constantly critical, and still, others are intentionally confrontational. These citizens, in many cases, make a point of refusing to be persuaded. This segment will teach you how to defuse awkward situations and win people over to your side.

SEPARATE AND CONQUER

When anyone sees you, they are filtered by the sense in which you all operate: their internal state as well as their personal and cultural filters. When you're working with a squad, it's far more challenging to have charisma because you have to manage all of the individual contexts on top of the group dynamic. When you're in the spotlight, it compensates for the multiple-context disadvantage. However, if you have a group of challenging people to persuade, working on each of them individually would give you a much better chance of success.

As we've seen, the "right" charisma style is determined by your personality, circumstance, your priorities, and the individual with whom you're interacting.

One circumstance might necessitate charismatic emphasis. Perhaps you're dealing with someone who wants to be heard and understood. Other times, authority or visionary charisma can be needed, such as when people are struggling with confusion and seeking a straightforward, convincing vision.

Consider the following suggestions to help convince whom you need to persuade and which styles may work better for each person once you've determined who you need to persuade.

CREATE THEM JUSTIFY YOUR POSITION IN YOUR FAVOUR.

How do you make the most of this technique? You may certainly enlist the assistance of your opponents or request a favour from them. Better still, ask them for something for which they will not be charged: their opinion. Asking for someone's opinion rather than their advice is a better approach because providing advice takes more time because they have to adapt a suggestion to the case while asking for their opinion allows them to say whatever they want.

The only way to get the advantages of rationalization is to use what they've already done for you. Find ways to thank them for any previous assistance they've given. Express your gratitude and appreciation, emphasize the decision they made and the effort they put in, and play up the fact that they put their name on the line for you in every way. It'll make them rationalize their behaviours in your favour, so keep that in mind.

APPRECIATION MESSAGES

Compliments that are both personal and precise are the most powerful and credible. Instead of saying "Nice work," say "You did a great job," or even better, "The way you held your cool when that client became obnoxious was amazing." The more you express gratitude and demonstrate the effect they've made on you, the more they'll like you and want to be a part of your success. They'll find a way to rationalize in your favour. People feel as if they've made you when you show them how they've influenced you. They develop a vested interest in you as a result of this sense of ownership, and you become a part of their identity. As a result, they feel a greater sense of responsibility for your performance.

Commercial airlines also use the classic marketing tactic of persuading people to rationalize in their favour.

Reminding someone that they had a choice and chose you, your business, your service, or your suggestion is one of the most effective ways to keep people's support for you or your idea going, particularly when things get tough and people start complaining.

Know that this mechanism works both ways, so don't make other people feel bad. When anyone thinks they have wronged you, they will try to justify their acts by convincing themselves that they were justified. They don't want to be seen as a bad guy, so you must have done something wrong for them to treat you this way. Few people, no matter how wrong they are, will blame themselves.

Not just for yourself, but even for the concept you're endorsing, you can use rationalization. When you show someone how much of an effect they've had on a project or an idea, they'll feel a sense of ownership and instinctively want to help it. Demonstrate it, and you'll be compelled to endorse it automatically. Demonstrate how it has improved as a result of their participation, decisions, or suggestions. The effect is manifested through change. We have made an impact as soon as we make a transition.

Show the individual how this concept or project was influenced by something they did in the past—a similar idea, project, or initiative they backed.

DO NOT ENTER UNPROTECTED.

Toxic individuals, like all toxic things, should be treated with caution. For your sake, not for theirs. Dealing with a challenging person, like any aggressive situation, will stimulate your stress system, causing adrenaline to flood your body, which can be fatal.

In short, hostile emotions can be harmful to your well-being if you don't know how to deal with them.

Instead of stress hormones flooding your system, which can affect mental function and trigger negative body language, flood your system with oxytocin. Get into empathy and remain there while working with a difficult person to do this. All of the compassion-accessing techniques you learned can be used. It's also worth considering that this individual may be in a deep state of self-loathing. Difficult people's internal worlds can be pretty nasty—why that's, they're difficult in the first place. Instead, if their emotional climate were one of harmony and love, they would radiate warmth. Hostility is often just the outward expression of internal chaos.

Consider an alternate universe if you're looking for a way to increase your compassion.

Remember, you're doing this for your own sake, not theirs. It will lower the body's toxicity level and make the process less frustrating for you. This technique can be used if you sense your frustration level rising.

Empathy will preserve your mental and emotional state while also providing you with the appropriate body language. This will be written over your face if you're in a combative mood. Empathy, on the other hand, would assist you in adopting a collaborative approach, giving you excellent body language and making the interaction even more manageable. This is why, when interacting with difficult people, kindness charisma can be a remarkably powerful weapon.

BRINGING BAD NEWS TO YOU

You won't always have control of when and where you have uncomfortable conversations. But, if you have the opportunity, think about both timing and venue. Take a moment to consider the person's emotional state before picking up the phone or sitting them down to chat.

If you know they've had a particularly trying, frustrating, or exhausting twenty-four hours and you have the time, wait a day.

Consider the atmosphere before breaking bad news, keeping in mind that people can pass their feelings about the environment to the experience itself. Choose a convenient place as much as possible. In a noisy environment, such as a train station or an airport, don't try to have a tough conversation.

Do whatever you can to make them feel more at ease. This can also be done with props. Have you ever noticed how people fidget with things in their hands or with their clothing—for example, toying with their shirt buttons when they're in the middle of a difficult conversation or when they're having trouble expressing themselves—when they're in the middle of a difficult conversation or when they're having trouble expressing themselves? They're deliberately looking for objects on which to concentrate their minds in order to divert their attention away from the pain of their current situation. Make it easy for them by keeping toys nearby with which they can play and thus feel more at ease when conversing with you. They won't know what's going on, but they'll notice that the conversation is becoming easier and more relaxed.

The beneficial distracting effect of candles and firelight is the same. This is why they're so common in romantic situations, where ease and comfort are essential. These constantly shifting elements give people the impression that something is going on in the background that they can focus on when they need a break. Of course, background music provides some of the same diversion.

When it comes to delivering bad news of some kind, your body language is crucial. Remember how positive performance reviews with positive body language were received much more than negative performance reviews with negative body language? Your body language has a much greater effect than your intense vocabulary circumstances. When the stress system kicks in, a more primitive portion of the brain takes over, one that doesn't understand words or concepts explicitly. Body language, on the other hand, has an immediate influence.

Warmth is the best body language to use when giving bad news: care, compassion, understanding, and empathy. Basically, show as much compassion and charm as you can. The more distressing the news, the more important it is for the receiver to know that you genuinely understand and are there for them. This is where goodwill, kindness, and empathy, which are internal instruments, come into play.

- Firstly, get yourself into the right internal state. Solicit sympathy and let it show in your body language.
- Put yourself in their shoes; imagine what it's like inside their mind, inside their life, in great detail. Imagine both of you wearing angel wings and working together on a common goal.
- Concentrate on a kind expression like "Just love as much as you can from wherever you are."
- Use facial expressions, tone of voice, and vocabulary to demonstrate empathy.

What kind of tough message you have to convey determines the appropriate verbal vocabulary to use when delivering bad news. In most situations, you can use the advice to make the message more applicable to them, such as using their words, analogies, and metaphors. Whether you're giving this post to a wider group of people, make sure you communicate your care and concern both nonverbally and verbally in your interaction; tell them, if possible, what you would like to do to alleviate their discomfort. Demonstrate that you are well aware of not just how unwelcome the news is but also the implications it may have for them.

Switch your kindness charisma not only toward them but also toward yourself in the experience. Use all of the internal resources you've learned to help you cope with this tough situation as best you can, and continue to praise and inspire yourself. You're giving it your all.

CRITICISM DELIVERED

Unfortunately, criticism is a necessary evil, much like dental tests, airport screening, and, depending on who you ask, taxes. You may not like it, but you have to do it sometimes. Someone will do something wrong at some point in your life, whether it's a parent, partner, friend, colleague, or boss, and you'll have to tell them about it. Of course, the question is how to do it properly.

When it comes to presenting criticism charismatically, there are four steps to follow.

Consider the timing and the venue first. When choosing between the two, try to be as empathic as possible. Consider the person's stress and exhaustion levels. Try to offer criticism (or "constructive feedback") as soon as possible after experiencing the action you want to improve. When you do so, make sure the person is in a physically and emotionally open state.

Second, adopt the appropriate attitude, which is one of compassion and empathy. Yes, even when giving feedback, your sensitivity can show in your body language and have a positive impact on the whole relationship. Warmth is also relevant in this situation. Kindness or concentration charisma will help to alleviate the problem, while authority charisma will make it worse.

It can completely shift the dynamic if people believe you are looking out for their best interests. You should also try imagining a person you admire right before you offer criticism to get into the right mental state. Consider a favourite grandparent, counsellor, spiritual figure, or someone else who means a lot to you. How would you phrase your criticism if you were to say it to them or in front of them? In what ways do you think your opinions are evolving now? Throughout the tough talk, try to remind yourself of this and imagine the esteemed mentor watching you.

Third, make a list of the points you want to make and be precise. Instead of making an exhaustive list, concentrate on a few key points to keep the other person from being frustrated. Furthermore, if your critique is too broad, their risk-averse brain can conjure up the worst possible interpretations of your message.

Depersonalization is the fourth step. As much as possible, make it clear that you're criticizing the action rather than the individual. When someone's motives or character qualities are questioned, it's more difficult to find common ground. Be cautious if your motives or personality characteristics have been questioned. Always be careful of thinking you know a person's true motivations.

Instead, concentrate on patterns that have been observed and evidence that have been tested.

Even if the criticism is directed at the action, try to keep it as impersonal as possible. Saying something like, "Why do you still procrastinate on presentations until the last minute?" is a bad idea. "This is both a personal and a generic statement.

DELIVERIES THAT ARE CRITICAL

You're ready to start charismatically providing the tough feedback now that you've considered timing and place and selected the precise, empathetically phrased points you want to make. It's critical to get off to a good start. The way you start the discussion will have a big impact on how people perceive it.

Humans have a strong memory for "firsts"—the first time anything occurs or the start of an experience—and we also have a strong memory for "lasts."

If you begin your critique with a positive note, the rest of the experience will be influenced. People need reassurance in the first few minutes when they are most fearful. You can give them a firm foundation by stating that you respect them—that you understand their value as human beings and that they matter to you as colleagues and clients.

People can consider your comments much more readily and become less defensive because they have been convinced of their own worth. Indeed, this move may be the most crucial in preventing a defensive reaction. After all, defensiveness is mostly only the outward manifestation of anxiety and insecurity.

Let's presume a colleague has been slacking on his responsibilities. Rather than bringing this up explicitly, consider his many positive achievements first. In this way, he can feel as if his whole life has been reasonably acknowledged. It also recognizes the behaviour as sporadic, a blip in otherwise excellent behaviour.

You should bring up the actual problem you want to fix once you've begun on a positive note. Tell people what you want to see from them, not what you don't want to see from them.

When you tell the person you're criticizing about the disciplinary action you want to see, depersonalize the behaviour improvement in the same way you depersonalized the criticism. Instead of saying, "Could you finish the presentation sooner?" say, "In the future, I'd greatly appreciate it if the presentation could be prepared a few days ahead of time." This removes the question of who was right and who was wrong from the equation and instead focused on something you can all agree on without someone having to win or lose.

When giving criticism, try to stop making people feel bad, just as you might when dealing with a difficult person. When someone is told they're wrong, even though they know they're wrong, they sometimes try to defend themselves; this can both wound their pride and arouse their anger, causing them and try to undermine you in order to minimize their own guilt.

"You know, I may not be explaining this the right way," you can tell in a similar vein. Allow me to try once more." Take the high road. When you're a charismatic communicator, other people feel good about themselves when they're around you. It means that people look forward to spending time with you because being around you makes them feel better about themselves.

Body language is important here, as it always is. With a look, intonation, or gesture, you can tell someone you think they're wrong just as well as you can with words. So make use of all of your resources to maintain an internal state of peace and goodwill.

You'll notice a change in your body language.

During difficult talks, it's important to remain alert for any signs that the other person is being defensive. If you notice defensiveness in their facial expressions, body language, or tone of voice, increase your warmth to help them return to a more optimistic mindset. This can be accomplished in two ways:

- Encourage constructive mental comparisons verbally. Mention something they've done in an awesome way in the past or something you approve of in this case, for example.
- **Nonverbally**: Manipulate their body language by using yours. Get back into a positive frame of mind so that it shows on your face. Their brain's mirror neurons will mimic the feelings they see in you, placing them in a more optimistic frame of mind.

If at all possible, try to finish the discussion on a positive note. Keep in mind how crucial beginnings and ends are—they can influence the whole relationship. This is the time to emphasize three main points:

- **Next steps**: Go through the steps you'll take to improve the situation, particularly if you'll be doing all of them together.

Give the impression that you're moving forward in a positive way.

- **Appreciation**: Express your gratitude for how well they responded to your suggestions. You're providing positive feedback here by praising even the tiniest good effort; you're providing positive reinforcement so they'll progress over time.
- **A bright future**: Mention something that both of you may look forward to in the future, such as fun activities or upcoming projects—whatever expresses your eagerness for future experiences.

WHAT TO DO WHEN THINGS GO WRONG: APOLOGIES

So you made a mistake. You pressed reply all by accident and didn't double-check the numbers. Whatever you want to call it, something bad has happened, and someone believes it is your fault, whether they are correct or not. Don't be concerned. Someone will blame you if you play incorrectly. Don't be concerned. Even embarrassing gaffes can be turned around if you play your cards right.

A disagreement or conflict can actually strengthen a relationship and be beneficial in the long run. When a relationship has started very well, there may be a lingering scepticism in the back of our minds. So far, everything has gone smoothly, but what if things change? What would their reaction be then? You know your relationship can withstand difficulty once you've successfully navigated a difficult situation. The apprehension has been dispelled.

First and foremost, as always, get into the proper mental frame of mind. First and foremost, this entails self-forgiveness. While it might seem counterintuitive, it is important to be warm toward yourself, even if you are at fault, in order to avoid exacerbating the situation by negative body language. It will greatly assist you in avoiding any defensive tone in your speech, stance, or facial expression. To access and maintain a state of self-compassion, use the resources we've discussed.

You may avoid appearing unnecessarily apologetic, subservient, or vulnerable by forgiving yourself and moving into a positive mental state. You can embody both comfort and contrition while also coming from a position of strength if you have the faith that comes with a healthy internal state.

Let's move on to the other individual now that you're in a good mental condition. You should aim for a personal touch the more serious the offence is. The person delivering the apology may need to see or hear the regret in your face or voice to be satisfied.

Since so much of our communication is nonverbal, you have the most resources at your disposal when you apologize in person: body language, facial gestures, and voice tone, in addition to the words you use. When you're on the phone, you just have your voice and words to deal with, and in an e-mail, you have even fewer options.

Some people, on the other hand, find that the distance provided by a written medium makes it easier to manage such challenging situations. Written correspondence has the benefit of allowing you to devote hours of thought to only a few lines of communication, ensuring that they are perfect. Putting something down on paper will make a strong point. In a way, you're committing to it; you're ready to be kept accountable.

As with so many of the charisma-enhancing strategies, the best match will depend on your tastes, your best guess of their preferences, and what the logistics, timing, and context allow.

LISTEN TO THEM.

Your first priority, whether you're apologizing in person or over the phone, is to give the other person the opportunity to talk. Listening is the easiest and most powerful way to do so: give them your full attention and charisma. I'm not suggesting that putting this into effect will be easy. You might have a dozen retorts ready for each complaint your counterpart makes. Interrupting is, however, the worst move you can make at this stage. They would feel belittled rather than accepted and understood, no matter how smart you are or how correct your rebuttal is.

Try not to prepare your answer while you listen. Instead, concentrate all of your efforts on deciding the exact nature of the issue. To ensure your understanding, ask questions.

IN THIS CASE, TOO, GOODWILL IS ESSENTIAL.

Simply approaching a discussion with the attitude of "Help me understand how you see things" will fully transform the result. The mere reality of being in an open mental stance has an effect on your speech, facial expressions, words used, and body posture, as well as the emotional tone of the conversation. Your goodwill is written all over your face and can be seen in any micro expression you make.

To inject warmth into the conversation, use some of the internal resources we've discussed, and invoke your kindness charisma. Consider holding your head down, eyes wide open, and voice warm and slow, with frequent pauses to allow the other person to jump in if they so desire.

Once you're certain you understand the complaint and accept that you're to blame, a genuine apology is in order. Surprisingly, the wording you use can be quite straightforward (again, body language is what really matters).

What counts is how compassionate you are, how concerned you are, and how personally involved you are. Saying "I'm sorry" rather than "Sorry" indicates that you personally agree with and are affected by the situation they're in. Sincerity is crucial: rather than just apologizing to calm them down, you must sound as if you really believe it.

Demonstrate that you are aware of both the direct and indirect effects of your acts (or inaction). In a business setting, you should demonstrate that you comprehend how this error affects their objectives or the performance of their company. Then show what you'll do to make it right or ensure it doesn't happen again. So, what are your plans? Make your statement as specific as you can.

And the most accomplished individuals make mistakes. Even missteps can become opportunities if you apply these concepts. These stressful encounters, when treated properly, can become bonding experiences, giving your relationships a new dimension.

E-MAIL AND PHONE

Phone and e-mail aren't enough when it comes to charisma. Communication presents a unique set of difficulties. A significant amount of nonverbal contact is clearly missed. You lose all visual contact when you're on the phone, and you lose all but words when you're communicating through e-mail. Furthermore, e-mail does not allow you to make mid-course adjustments based on the other person's answer.

The key principles, however, remain valid: consider the timing, environment, and condition in which the individual may be. To strengthen with practice, plan the order in which you send e-mails and make phone calls, starting with the least significant. You can also use visualizations to get into the right mental state before important calls and e-mails so that the appropriate words and tone flow naturally.

Pay attention after you've joined a discussion. Since you have fewer visual cues (such as body language) to decipher and must rely solely on auditory signals, you must be as concentrated as though you were face-to-face—perhaps even more so. Concentrate and maintain silence. Do you believe you should eat, drink, or use your machine while on the phone? And don't jump to conclusions. It's forbidden to eat or drink. Since receivers are specifically designed to enhance the sound, even if you think you're silent, the individual will hear you chewing and swallowing. People will almost certainly hear you type and wonder what you're thinking about.

Reading e-mail or browsing the Web is also not a good idea— it can cause a slight pause in your answer time, making you seem as if your mind is wandering.

Delayed vocal responses may have the same effect as facial movements that are delayed. Your diversion can manifest itself if your mind wanders. It's just as important to be present on the phone as it is in person. Because of the ways you can connect, it's often easier to project presence in person. For it to be answered over the internet, you have to work that much harder.

Remove yourself from all distractions and get up from your desk for the best performance. Stay standing and walk about (this will make the voice sound more energized) while concentrating solely on the phone call.

Pay attention to what the other person is doing as well as the background noises. If the other phone line rings, ask if he wants to answer it and reassure him that all is fine. You don't want his mind to be divided between vaguely listening to you and trying to find out who the other caller is.

All of the techniques and concepts you learned in the previous sections can be applied while writing e-mails. Review a couple of the principles you've learned so far. Examine some of your previous e-mails. When compared to the word you, how often does the word I appear? Is the first part of the e-mail about you and your hobbies? Don't resist your innate inclination (after all, we're hardwired to prioritize our own needs). Instead, write the e-mail as usual, but before sending it, cut and paste all that pertains to the other person first and foremost.

This can also be done with your marketing materials, such as your website, brochures, or anything else that represents you or your business to the outside world.

CHAPTER ELEVEN

PRESENTING WITH CHARISMA

Several charismatic public speaking forms are used in charismatic public speaking. This section will teach you how to:

- Use visionary charisma to create an exciting and motivating presentation.
- Use authority and charm to command the audience's attention and appreciation.
- Use compassion and charisma to connect with your audience.

If you're giving a presentation to a small group or a big one, the following tips apply. In reality, these rules are especially useful when you're trying to encourage, influence, or convince a single person. If you're giving a keynote speech at a conference or pitching a new business idea to your boss, the techniques mentioned below will help you craft your message, choose your words, and refine your delivery until your presentations are literally irresistible.

PUTTING TOGETHER A CHARISMATIC MESSAGE

Most of us use presentations to persuade others of something—a concept, an initiative, or a course of action. Though we'll go through a wide range of charismatic communications tactics, it all starts with understanding who we're trying to convince.

You, too, will often communicate with attention-starved viewers who will only pay attention to a portion of what you say. If you can keep this one detail in mind while you're speaking, you'll be fine. You'll be more successful than 80% of the speakers out there if you keep this one truth in mind when crafting your presentation and designing your speech accordingly.

Choose the most important concept you want to communicate and make it as straightforward and simple to understand as possible. Your message should ideally be able to be expressed in a single sentence.

Have three to five primary supporting points inside this one main post. The human brain works in triads and cannot comprehend numbers greater than four right away. Opening each of your supporting points with amusing anecdotes, interesting details, convincing numbers, fantastic metaphors, illustrations, and analogies is a good idea.

People are especially influenced by stories. In reality, viewers always remember the story first, then the argument the story was trying to make. People have been telling stories as a means of transmitting knowledge to one another since the beginning of time.

To make your stories more relatable and engaging (and short!), use characters that are close to the people in your audience. If you realize it or not, you're in the entertainment industry when you give a presentation. As a result, it makes the story exciting. You're appealing to visionary charisma, which, like all types of charisma, involves appealing to people's emotions.

Using metaphors and analogies to capture the audience's imagination can be very powerful. Choose photos and analogies that will cater to a young audience for optimum effect. Speeches that refer to our childhood origins are the ones that make us feel awe and wonder. If you're talking about your customer base's untapped potential, compare yourself to "bounty hunters" or "treasure hunters" looking for "hidden gold."

Also, statistics and figures can be made intimate, relevant, and relatable to your audience. r you willing to go to the moon and back?"

Make sure you end with a clear point or a transition to the action step you want your audience to take, whether you use a plot, example, number, or statistic. Remember to provide a call to action for your audience. Remember to keep things as clear as possible so that even multitasking, partly listening audience member can understand it.

Bear in mind that we remember beginnings and ends the most when crafting your presentation's closing. Avoid finishing with Q&A because, just as you want to start on a high note, you want to finish on a high note as well. It's difficult to have a question and answer session that's as engaging and enthralling as your main expression. The Q&A cycle almost always depletes the electricity.

You can begin crafting your sentences once you've completed your structure. The following pointers will assist you in choosing your words:

• They are the centre of attention. As much as possible, use the term you. Make use of their sentences, tales, and metaphors. Also, try to adapt your verbs to your audience: for business people, lead or initiate; for engineers, build; and for artists, craft.

• Create a graphic. Since the brain thinks in pictures, use vibrant, sensory-rich language.

• When negotiating, be wary of the "no issue" trap.

• Keep it brief. Consider the following questions for each sentence: What meaning does this sentence provide? Even when writing stories, only provide information that helps the reader understand or enjoy the story. Consider a sneak peek rather than a full-length film.

DEVELOPING A CHARISMATIC PRESENCE

Since you'll be the centre of attention, consider the message you want to send through your clothes. Is it a matter of authority? What does it mean to have power? Is there any warmth? Consider what social scientists have discovered about chromatic effects:

- The colour red is associated with vigour and passion. To arouse an audience, wear red.
- Wearing black demonstrates that you're serious and won't take no for an answer.
- In the courtroom, white exudes integrity and innocence, which is why defendants always choose it. The colour blue is associated with confidence. The deeper the shadow, the higher the degree of confidence it inspires.
- Gray is a strong neutral and the quintessential business hue.
- Avoid the colours orange and purple. They are the first to draw the human eye's attention, but they are often the first to wear it out.

You must be physically confident in order to project trust and move with ease on stage. Make sure nothing is impeding your movements, impairing your equilibrium, or reducing your relaxation in any way. It's difficult enough to feel completely at ease on stage when alone in front of an audience, let alone dealing with physical discomfort! This entails wearing clothing that allows you to breathe and secure shoes. Your brain's first job is to keep an eye on your safety, whether that means avoiding predators or staying upright. If it has to focus all of its attention on your breathing or equilibrium, it can't devote at least some of it to your speaking performance. Why squander some of your concentration?

PRACTISING FOR CHARISMA

When you know a presentation can have a huge effect on your future, it's worth practising until you like it's ingrained in your bones. Magicians use an interesting trick in which they run through the entire show once with their eyes closed.

Another good idea is to record or videotape your speech and count what experienced speakers refer to as irritants. Any sounds or gestures that do not contribute to your message are considered distractions. Every sound and facial expression you create is a means of communication that demands a portion of the audience's attention because they are watching your every move. Be strategic: make sure each nonverbal gesture you make adds meaning and minimizes superfluous movements to avoid wasting any of your audience's time.

Ask people to point out any unnecessary movements, tics, or disruptions if you've been videotaped. Don't do it yourself—much it's harder to hear our own irritants, and recording services are inexpensive. If you've been audiotaped, get the voice transcribed and ask them to remember every "um" and "ah."

Perform the entire speech in front of a live audience at least once as a practice run. When you deliver the same knowledge to real, breathing people, the dynamics shift radically, no matter how much you've practised your presentation on your own.

PROJECTING STRENGTH

Speakers who are charismatic know how to give the appearance that they are as at ease walking across the stage as they are in their own living room. This is known as "owning the stage," and it can be accomplished in three ways.

To begin, make sure you have a wide stance and are well balanced on both feet when you stand. You will not only feel more secure, but you will also be more balanced on both feet. You'll not only feel more secure, but you'll also seem more confident and steady than if you stood on one foot. Wide, stable stances also aid in trust projection.

Second, practice speaking without the use of a podium or lectern. Speaking behind one might give the impression that you're afraid to go outside and want to stay safe behind a shield. The presentation becomes even more static as a result of this. Consider the stereotypical lecturer who sits immobile at his lectern, reading from his notes in a monotone voice. You can appear much more confident, powerful, and charismatic if you move around the stage with ease.

Third, determine the appropriate volume to convey trust. This is difficult because so much depends on the microphone you're given that day and the sound system's configuration. Ask a few people in the back of the room to be your sound experts just before the speech and give you a prearranged signal to increase or lower your volume if necessary.

Warmth Projection

Though this might seem excessive in the comfort of one's own home or office, the situation is very different on stage. Your brain speeds up in the heat of battle, with adrenaline coursing through your veins. This is why everything around you may appear to be moving slowly. You'll talk more quickly as the brain goes into hyperdrive. Your crowd, on the other hand, is always moving at a regular pace.

In addition to training, having a member of the audience send you a pre-arranged signal encouraging you to slow down may be beneficial.

It's important to pay attention to your pace because the slower you talk, the more reflective and deliberate you sound, and the more people will pay attention to what you're saying.

Pause often and purposefully in your voice. Have the courage to make your audience wait for you to say something. A dramatic delay is called that for a reason: it creates suspense.

Pause for a few seconds after presenting the main point of telling an engaging story to allow your audience to absorb it. Have the patience to wait for the laughter to swell and subside before moving on if you've already used humour. It's necessary to pause at the start and end of your speeches. Come to the middle of the stage, face the crowd, and come to a complete stop. Maintain total silence when counting three full seconds and steadily running your gaze through the crowd, making eye contact. This will seem interminable, but it will be well worth the effort. This kind of silence holds an audience's attention like nothing else. Ending the presentations with a pause is equally essential. Don't dart off the stage.

Corrections in the middle of the race

Consider yourself in the middle of a presentation when you make a mistake. You stutter, say the wrong thing, miss the point, or actually lose track of what you're saying.

You risk triggering your fight-or-flight answer if you let your internal critic take over and start berating you for it. Your body will switch off "unnecessary" functions like your brain's ability to think rationally, which is probably the last thing you want in that situation. So, what are your options?

Aim for a fast perspective change if you caught the vital thoughts before the accompanying emotions completely blossomed (rewriting your reality). Even seeing the error you made as a positive thing for a second can be enough to stop the fight-or-flight response in its tracks. Since the brain's first response to new ideas is to embrace them as true, you'll have already passed forward with renewed faith in the extra second it takes for disbelief to emerge.

You can convince yourself, for example, that corporate leaders and entertainers deliberately make mistakes to make themselves more relatable to the audience.

To turn off the fight-or-flight reflex, you'll need to flood your body with oxytocin if negative feelings have already surfaced.

CHAPTER TWELVE

30 DAYS' ACTION PLAN

The exercises below will take between 2 and 20 minutes to read and complete. The first ones are longer, while the later ones are shorter. Before going to work or school, you can include this time in your morning routine.

Then you'll go out and spend the rest of the day thinking about that particular exercise.

Don't bother if you're just going to skim through these. It'd be like reading through a workout routine and hoping to wake up the next day feeling better.

Commit to spending (at most) 20 minutes on these each morning. For a period of 30 days, Make a commitment to applying what you've learned each day to all of your experiences. If you do so, you will see results much more quickly than if you were lifting weights in the gym. The outcomes would be immediate in some situations.

DAY 1: LAYING THE GROUNDWORK

So, get a piece of paper and a pen, or open a text document, and get started. On a scale of 1 to 10, rate your level of belief in each of the charismatic mindsets (1 being no belief at all, 10 being complete belief). Tell the truth of where you are RIGHT NOW.

1. I'm fine. I'll be fine.
2. My character is more important to me than other people's views.
3. I am a person of impeccable moral character.
4. I don't need to persuade anybody
5. I'm willing to go first in.
6. Having a good time
7. Tapping into taboo topics
8. Establishing simple lines of demarcation
9. Breaking down physical obstacles
10. Complimenting others
11. Being honest about my faults
12. I show when I'm frustrated, nervous, or hurt
13. I have a purpose, and I share it

Did you assign a number from 1 to 10 to each of these? That's great. Now that you've done that write down what not believing has cost you if your score is less than a ten.

Now I'd like to write down what you'd benefit from if you ranked each conviction from one to ten. What incredible feats would you be able to accomplish? What would people think about you if they saw you? What will they think? What does that mean for your personal life and professional life? Per belief, allow 30-60 seconds. Simply put, write. Let's go!

Now, out of those, choose the ONE that would have the greatest effect if you multiplied it by ten. The one that is depriving you of the things you want. The one from which you stand to benefit the most.

Don't worry if you don't know which one to choose. If you want, you can complete them all later. For the time being, just pick the best belief, to begin with.

Did you choose your charismatic frame of mind? That's great!

This is your today's project attitude!

This is the one you'll be focusing on today. To begin, make a list of all the reasons you have to believe it. I'm fine.

Ninety seconds of writing You have every reason to believe in the charismatic mentality. Let's go!

You should now have some compelling reasons to hold the conviction. You're probably more secure in that attitude now than you were just a few minutes ago because you shifted your attention. It's now up to you to completely internalize it.

To do so, we're going to act silly. What exactly do I mean?

Any time you're unsure how to behave for the rest of the day, ask yourself, "What would I do if I kept my project attitude at a ten?" If you're not doing it, ask yourself, "What can I do to act more like this?" My project trust is a ten.

This will necessitate bravery. You'll realize you need to speak to that intimidating person, assert yourself where you've previously been silent, tell the people closest to you when they've hurt you, or, more challenging, tell them how valuable they are. This challenge's success DOES NOT LOOK LIKE PERFECTION in living the projected attitude at a ten on a scale of 1-10. Success is becoming aware of your desire to strengthen your belief. When you see yourself behaving in a way that isn't in line with it, it's time to change direction.

Also, remember to save the paper you worked on! We'll go over it again later.

DAY 2: GETTING RID OF NON-CHARISMATIC TENDENCIES (EYES)

Your task for the day is to talk while looking people in the eyes.

For certain people, this is going to be very difficult. It will be difficult for you to remember. You'll most likely want to turn away.

Don't do it. Get in the habit of making eye contact while chatting. You want to get to the stage where you want to break eye contact rather than feeling compelled to do so because you're nervous.

This should be done for everybody. Anyone you talk with: family, friends, cashiers, etc. There's no need to inform them. That will only increase their anxiety.

Don't worry if you have trouble at first. It's similar to lifting weights. The effects aren't visible on the first day. This habit, however, will change your relationships in just a few weeks. Good eye contact has the power to transform people's lives.

There are various schools of thought as to where to look.

Some would advise you to look at the bridge of the listener's nose.

Some people recommend picking one eye and moving it back and forth.

You have the option of focusing on one eye or using a soft gaze that allows you to see both eyes. Do not look at someone's bridge of the nose. Look away from their brow. This defeats the intent of reaching out to them in the first place.

Carry on like this for the remainder of the day. Maintain constant eye contact with everyone, especially while speaking.

Now comes the tricky part: how do you maintain eye contact without frightening people?

The key is to have "narrow eyes." They're just as they say on the tin. By stimulating the muscles around the eye, you can keep the eyes a little narrower than when they're fully relaxed.

DAY 3: SMILING

Smiling is the region of most people's charm that has the most immediate effect.

If you're not a naturally cheerful person, this can be unsettling at first. Keep in mind that this is a test. We're determining the appropriate sum for you. Which, in the vast majority of instances, would be more enthusiastic and lively.

Here's what you have to do for the rest of the day: At the start of a conversation, smile at everyone you meet.

Is it true that everyone? Everyone, indeed.

When you're walking down the street, smile at the people, you encounter. When you greet coworkers, look them in the eyes. When you get home from work, go to your girlfriend, partner, husband, or wife.

You'll undoubtedly miss a few passers-by. The main thing is to remember this and make an honest attempt to smile at as many people as possible. You'll see how important smiling is at the start of a conversation and how to adjust yours for the best results.

DAY 4: CREATING A POSITIVE FIRST IMPRESSION

Introducing yourself is the most common contact you'll ever have. After all, even your closest friends were once strangers!

So, if you want to attract great people into your life, you must master this aspect of the relationship. What's more ridiculous is that 99 per cent of the time, this aspect of the interaction is dull and uninteresting!

So it might be worth putting in a little more effort, right?

Here's how to do it:

1. Take the lead in the discussion. People aren't interested in one-word answers. Give them 2-5 sentences to answer, so they have something to think about.
2. Disrupt established trends. Respond in a way that jolts people out of their routine.
3. Have a good time. Let people laugh and smile.
4. Tell us something interesting about yourself, like your motivations and beliefs.

You'll have a dynamite answer if you apply those four principles to every question you get.

By far the quickest way to make consistently great first impressions.

DAY 5: SHARING A STORY

We're going to focus on storytelling today. Anything we've done so far still applies.

- Strong eye contact is needed.
- The level of energy should be high. Speak with authority.

- We're currently working on a piece that tells a story, so emotion is at the forefront.
- Make a map of your emotional journey.
- Consider a story you've previously heard. We'll make certain you say it in the most effective way possible.
- Ask yourself, "Why am I telling this story?" as a first move.
- Because it's amusing? Because it's startling? Because it's ridiculous?
- Suppose you can't think of a reasonable excuse, makeup one! Nobody wants to hear meaningless tales that only help to establish prestige.

What is the most important event you want to discuss? What kind of emotion is it meant to elicit?

Give the emotional journey a name. Maybe it's the transition from sadness to happiness. Maybe it's the ever-increasing absurdity. Summarize the tale in terms of the feelings it can elicit. All are built around your emotional direction once you've defined it.

DAY 6: VOICE

First and foremost, we must provide a benchmark in order to determine what can be improved.

To begin, turn on your computer or camera. Make a 2-minute recording of yourself speaking in response to the following prompt:

Excellent. It's time to take a look at yourself and give yourself a grade. On a scale of 1 to 10, with one being the worst and ten being the best, rate your:

- The use of filler words/silence (a lot of ums, uhs, or likes, or just dead air time?)

- Cadence control (Did you go too far, or did you vary the cadence to create intrigue?)
- Disturbance (louder is better up until the point where you are shouting)
- Tonal range (Did you have a monotone or varied tone?)
- Exuberance and vigour (Did you sound ecstatic while discussing the exciting parts?)
- Timbre (Did you have a deep voice?)

Choose one region in which you'd like to change. For the time being, avoid using a natural voice deepness. That comes from doing an exercise on a regular basis. For the time being, choose some of the others.

- Now write down your answer to the same prompt: "Can you tell me about your favourite day of your life?" "(you can pick the same day or a different one to mix things up)
- Once it's done, rewind it and rank yourself in the following categories:
- The use of filler words/silence (a lot of ums, uhs, or likes, or just dead air time?)
- Cadence control (Did you go too far, or did you vary the cadence to create intrigue?)
- Disturbance (louder is better up until the point where you are shouting)
- Tonal range (Did you have a monotone or varied tone?)
- Exuberance and vigour (Did you sound ecstatic while discussing the exciting parts?)
- Deepness of speech that is normal

Did you notice a difference? It's also surprising how easily you can progress if you simply recognize a problem and then focus on resolving it.

The aim now is to apply this progress in the real world. So, for the rest of the day, in every discussion, but focus on the one speaking field you'd like to change. So, whatever it is for you, you'll be speaking louder and eliminating filler terms.

Start wearing a rubber band on one wrist to serve as a reminder. You simply turn to the other wrist when you realize you've neglected to pay attention to your improvement location. This is a highly successful tactic because it serves as a constant reminder of your speaking objectives.

DAY 7: INCANTATIONS

We're going to create an incantation today. Since these can be amusing, they have their own day. There will be no skipping this way. You'll notice a significant change in your mood.

Here are the steps you can take;

The first step is to pick an emotion you'd like to experience. I'd suggest a mixture of energized, relaxed, and lively.

If you know what you're feeling? Make a name for it. It's best if you use a phrase you're familiar with.

Then, recall a time when you really felt that way. What role were you in? What were you doing with your face? How did your body language vary from where it is now? Assume those biomechanics for a moment (body language, posture, facial expressions). Perhaps you smile while opening your chest and lifting your chin.

If you're stuck for anything to do with your body, imagine somebody you meet who represents the emotion you've chosen. How would they react if they were completely immersed in that sensation? Assume the biomechanics of that human.

This is fantastic. "What expression encapsulates this feeling?" you may wonder." How can you pronounce the word in a different tone of voice? If you don't know right away, concentrate on preserving biomechanics. Keep the grin on your face. You'll remember the expression.

Make sure you repeat the process again (even better if you pick a time when you can use a boost). Getting in the habit of controlling your emotional state is a big step toward retaining charisma in any case.

DAY 8: GET READY

This will almost certainly necessitate some shopping. Feel free to postpone this to a weekend or a day when you'll be able to visit a store (in person is better if you're unsure how things fit). Simply go to Day 9 and return to this day the next time you have a chance to shop.

This isn't a style guide in the traditional sense. As a result, I'll keep this short.

Let's start with the formula for good attire:

You make an impression based on your clothes, background, and the subjective prejudice of onlookers.

Take a moment to absorb the formula. It's the secret to figuring out what kind of thin slice you have.

But you can't just put on a suit and call it a day if you want to make a good impression.

Here's a quick rundown:

Make a decision on which bucket you want to be in.

You're going to be thrown into a puddle. A businessman, a rock star, a fashionista, a slob, a regular guy, and so on.

Begin here. "How would I like to be perceived?" you might wonder." Look for the most trendy model for your bucket list.

Consider the person that you believe best represents the impact you want to make.

You can also use Google Images to find them.

You now know what kind of clothing you'll need. One last thing to think about if you're going to buy...

Still, always, always, always, always, always, always, always, always, always, always, always

DAY 9: EXPANSIVENESS AND TRANSPARENCY IN GESTICULATIONS

Today, I'm going to show you something that will help you become a more engaging speaker while also making you feel more dynamic.

While you're speaking, make big gestures!

For today, we'll just be adding one new gesture to your arsenal. It's best to choose one that extends outside the usual comfort zone.

That is, if you usually just move your hands when talking, choose something that requires you to use your whole forearm. Choose a motion that requires you to stretch your whole arm if you just shift your forearms from the elbow down.

Choose only one gesticulation to use for the remainder of the day. Decide what emotion it best conveys (is it for emphasis? to demonstrate certainty?) and use it wherever possible.

DAY 10: PLAYING AROUND

Today is all about having a good time!

Isn't it amusing? That thing we adore but never seem to find time for in our lives. Today is the day to change that. However, there is a catch...

An optimistic, fun-loving attitude isn't something you can turn on and off like a faucet. You might try, but you'll end up with jerky results. So, what are your options?

Have a good time with everyone!

It seems to be self-evident. However, it's likely that you have a number of people in your life whom you regard solemnly. Perhaps your coworkers. Perhaps the cashier at your favourite coffee shop. Or the building's doorman, who greets you with a curt "Good morning" or "Good night" depending on the time of day.

The genuinely charismatic person does not wait for a "huge fish" to enter the room before turning it on. That person has a charismatic personality. And it all begins with the mundane experiences they have on a daily basis.

So today's aim is to "mess about" with the families, colleagues, and service people you encounter.

Today, make it your mission to make people laugh and smile. Make a fool of yourself.

DAY 11: MAKE MORE DIRECT EYE CONTACT

It's time to resurrect something that had fallen by the wayside.

That will be done on a regular basis to strengthen skills.

That means (yet again!) it's all about eye contact today.

Recall what the charismatic gaze seems to be. Examine yourself in the mirror and make those slightly squinty eyes. Determine which point appears to be the most articulate and intense. That's the one you'll want to use in social situations.

The aim is simple: keep eye contact with anyone you talk to for the rest of the day. Maintain the charismatic gaze while adding a few gestures. A head tilt, a brow raise, or an eye smile are all examples of this.

DAY 12: TOUCHING

We'll be touching today.

That's the gist of it: contact people when you communicate with them. This could be on the arm, shoulder, a chest pat (only for guys!), a back clap, or touching the knee while you're both sitting.

Hover's hands are different from touching in that they occur when you place your hand over someone as though you're about to touch them but then decide it's not necessary.

There is a problem when touching becomes darting. Those lightning-quick touches can feel like an assault. The lingering contact, on the other hand, can make people uncomfortable. So, how much time do you spend touching?

The frontal touches will take one second. A back clap could take up to two seconds. A side hug can be awkward if it lasts longer than 3-5 seconds.

You're going about things the wrong way if you're doing it according to a map. Today's aim is to begin developing your own touching intuition. Regardless of prior conditioning that said, "Don't touch anybody!" So play around with it. You have permission to make mistakes.

Touch differs depending on the degree of familiarity – with the doorman; you'll usually stick to a handshake or shoulder pat. To make a point with a coworker, do the knee touch while both of you are sitting.

The whole point of charismatic touching is that different levels of contact build different levels of intimacy. Depending on how you touch them, they can feel closer to you. So make good use of it. Although you may want to increase your touching with the attractive person you're flirting with, you should be mindful that if you're not interested, too much touching will send the wrong signals. You'll have to go out and see how conversational dynamics change when the touching is added to the mix.

So, your aim for the day is to make an impression on everyone you meet! A forearm touch is perfect in passing conversations where you don't know who you're talking about. Experiment with various types of touching with people with whom you have different degrees of intimacy. This will improve your social instincts, allowing you to optimize your charismatic impact through contact.

DAY 13: POSITIVITY

Today, we're going to ramp up positivity. This is as much about making you feel great as it is about spreading the feeling to the rest of the world.

The following are the three primary tenants:

1. When you walk into a room, smile. When you meet new people, smile. When speaking to them, smile with your eyes.

2. Be ecstatic.

3. Just show support for others. There will be no cynical jokes.

Your ambition for today is to make others happy just by being present. To raise them up with your positive energy. If people wonder why you're so energetic or say you're in an especially good mood, you've done well. (Hint: If you're feeling down, use your incantation to re-energize yourself.)

DAY 14: A LOOK BACK AT CHARISMATIC MINDSETS

Can you recall those enthralling convictions? All of your micro-movements are guided by them. So, though thinking about the nuances of eye contact, laughing, and touching is beneficial, we're going to repeat the exercise from the first day, this time with a different conviction.

So go over the sheet again and consider which other belief will have the most effect if you increased it to a ten (pick a different one than you did on the first day). This is the one you'll be focusing on today. So, right now, rewrite all of the excuses you do have to believe it.

DAY 15: ASSESS YOUR INTEGRITY AND TRUSTWORTHINESS.

This is an excellent time to do some of the more in-depth charismatic jobs.

It's all about personality. It's all about confidence.

Charisma is a sense of ease in the presence of others. When we sense that someone is genuine, we get a sense of it. We have faith in their behaviour and believe we can let down our barriers with them. We have confidence in them and their motives.

Honesty is the bedrock of that faith. First and foremost, honesty with oneself. Then there's the rest of the planet. But that's what we're going to talk about today. Consider the following questions:

Where have I been untruthful to myself or to others?

Are there any issues that I haven't addressed?

Have I changed my mind in order to appease those around me?

Have I made any promises that I haven't followed through on? Promises I'm not going to keep?

Finding the places where you might be destroying trust is the first step in building trust—the places where you aren't completely truthful. Then you cease to deceive. You alter your actions so that your words and actions are in sync.

If you secretly harbour animosity toward others, either let it go or talk to them about it.

If you're not keeping promises, you either stop making them or start keeping them, even if it's inconvenient.

If you're deceptive, choose your position before the pressure is applied and reflect it correctly, no matter who is present.

And always sound as if the person you're talking to is present.

Today, increase your knowledge of your integrity. Make no promises that you won't be able to keep. Keep all of your promises. Often, don't cheat in order to get what you want.

DAY 16: GENUINE COMPLIMENTS

That includes going first when it comes to expressing what they admire in others, what they find admirable. It entails making sincere compliments without any preconceived notions.

It can't be for the sake of gaining favour—compliment people who you want to like, not people who you want to like. Simply say out loud the pleasant thoughts that come to mind.

Today's aim is to be more precise with your compliments.

Compliments can range in size from large to small. They may be about clothing items or personality characteristics. The goal is to develop the habit of saying nice things to others in a way that makes them feel good.

DAY 17: THERE WILL BE NO FILLER TERMS.

Consider the first time we did a speech baseline. Did you depend on any verbal aids? When you were dreaming, you might have said something like "uhh" or "Ummm." Maybe you always say "honestly" when you make a comment.

You're going to get rid of your crutches today and replace them with nothing.

Slow down if you hear yourself saying any of those crutch terms. Speak at a rate that allows you to monitor the sounds that come out of your mouth. The majority of filler words would vanish simply by drawing your attention to them.

DAY 18: TURN UP THE VOLUME.

People who are charismatic appear to talk louder than others. Not at the expense of others. Just a little louder. They trust in the validity of their speech. When they talk, they make a loud noise that alerts others to pay attention.

Today, let's concentrate on two things:

1. Speak more loudly than normal. If other people can hear your conversation when you're anxious, you're doing it right.

2. Don't go off on a tangent. Finish your sentences at the same volume as you began them.

DAY 19: WHAT IS CAUSING YOU STRESS?

How you feel has a lot to do with your charisma. It flows easily if you are free, optimistic, and stress-free. Exuding charisma becomes a chore if you are preoccupied and tense.

So, ask yourself if there's something that's been bothering you recently. Do you find yourself in a financial bind? Are you worried about a major project at work? Is there a friendship that you're having trouble with? Do you worry that you're not charismatic enough?

Consider this: has there been something bothering me today or in the last few days?

Consider one thing, even though it is insignificant. Perhaps there is a source of stress in your life. Perhaps you've been harbouring a negative feeling about others.

Do you think you'll look back on this and wish you'd been more concerned about it when you're lying on your deathbed? Are you going to regret holding on to those negative emotions? Or would you wish you had seen your issues for what they were: roadblocks, hurdles, and opportunities to show off your best qualities?

Keep in mind that everything will turn out well. Holding on to your tension makes you vulnerable and less charismatic.

DAY 20: VOCAL RANGE

We recently increased the frequency of your speaking speech. We're now going to add variety.

It can be difficult to break out of your usual range. The best advice I can offer is to give yourself permission to experiment for one day. Make the most of it. Consider a kindergarten teacher who reads to the children. Consider how enthralled she is and how her tone shifts to match the emotion of the words she reads. For today, talk as if the instructor were reading.

Throughout the day, pay attention. Is it true that people are more enthralled by what you have to say? People are more shut-in when you tell them stories? What facial expressions or inflexions tend to make people laugh the loudest? Who has the most concentrated attention?

DAY 21: MESSING AROUND (AGAIN!)

Today's post is a refresher on tinkering, which is at the core of the charismatic discussion. Pay special attention to those who provide services. People that most people regard as robots are doormen, cab drivers, cashiers, and waiters. Make every effort to make them laugh and smile. This entails being amusing, laughing at them, and cracking jokes while you place your order. Talk with a silly lisp. Whatever makes you and everyone around you happy.

DAY 22: PUTTING THE SPOTLIGHT ON OTHERS

With all of the practice in eye contact, tonality, body language, and mindsets, you should have made some significant progress by this point. Now that your deeds have drawn attention to you, it's time to turn the spotlight back on others.

As a result, I have become genuinely curious about other people today. Go on a quest to learn everything there is to know about them. Listen to someone as if you're going to run into them again. That means you'll pay extra attention to remembering people's names when you encounter new people. You'll inquire about things other than the standard, "Where are you from?" "What do you do?" because you're curious about the fascinating information. You'll inquire about how they like their work and what they're looking forward to. With regular eye contact and smiles, you'll show them you care. Spend the day expressing your sincere interest in others to the extreme.

DAY 23: POSTURE

Make your way to a full-length mirror. Undress to your underwear. Close your eyes and move your body around. Then, when you're standing normally and comfortable, open your eyes.

People suffer from a variety of posture problems. Fixing them all properly might be a whole book in and of itself. The corrections to the two most popular ones I see are mentioned below.

Will you be able to hold two pens in your fists and have them point in the same direction? Or will the arrow be pointing inward? This is something you can actually do and check.

If you're looking inward, it means your chest is larger than your back. It may lead to a hunched stance or shoulders that are facing forward.

To correct this, stretch your shoulders and pecs while strengthening your back to bring your shoulders back naturally.

Does it kick out when you look at your pelvis and butt? An anterior pelvic tilt is very common in people who spend the majority of their days sitting. It's caused by poor glutes, hamstrings, and abdominals, as well as tight hip flexors (the front of your leg) and back extensors (your lower back). Crush your butt cheeks together while stimulating your heart and dragging your abs along your spine to get a sense of what proper posture looks like. The pelvis should be tilted in a different direction.

You won't be able to correct your posture forever in a single day. However, after reading this, you should have a better understanding of what it means to "stand up straight" when entering an important meeting.

DAY 24: INSANELY GOOD EYE CONTACT

This is something you've seen before. So take this as a friendly note. After all, repetition is the mother of all skills.

When speaking, maintain eye contact. I mean, I know, it's from a long time ago. But it comes up very much because it is such a simple ability to neglect. And by letting it slip, we're signalling to the rest of the planet that we don't want them to pay attention.

But today, pay extra attention to your eye contact. Only a friendly reminder:

1. Keep a slight squint on your face.
2. Make an eye-catching smile (can be activated by incantations or just genuinely feeling happy).
3. When you're speaking, pay close attention to your eye contact. This is the most common time for people to lose attention.

DAY 25: GESTICULATIONS, STANCE, AND TOUCHING

It's time to assemble the whole body. Today, there will be three main points of focus:

1. Extensively gesticulate. It's not a good idea to have your guns by your sides. If you find yourself limited to small movements, try the Vitruvian Man stretch.

2. As soon as you notice a problem with your stance, correct it. This entails sitting and standing in a straight position. If you discovered personal problems, it might also mean pushing your head back or fixing a pelvic tilt. When you step into a room, pay careful attention to your posture because this is when people notice you the most.

3. Make eye contact during a conversation. Shoulder claps, back pats, and forearm touches are all good options.

Today, let your body do the charismatic work for you. If you're speaking, listening, or simply walking, make a major impression.

DAY 26: TAKE IT EASY ON YOURSELF.

We've come to the end of the road. There's still a lot of work to be done in terms of analysis. But there's one more thing I'd like to bring up. Speaking is a verb. Slower is the term.

This isn't the most important update. In contrast to eye contact and gesticulations, many people talk at a pace that is perfectly acceptable for charisma. It can, however, be a game-changer for some fast talkers.

Enable your speech rate to slow down today. You can also record a standard rate of speech and then a version that is 50 per cent lower if you like. Then watch both of them and decide which one you prefer.

When you're slowing down your speech today, pay special attention to filler terms. Remove them from the image. Allow space between your thoughts for quiet. And, if you need some more convincing, slow speech can be engrossing.

DAY 27: INCANTATIONS AND ENERGY

Today, it's all about the fundamentals! But this time, I'm going to combine them in a powerful way.

Can you recall what your incantation was? What would you say to yourself to get yourself in a good mood? You're going to put that to use today to help you add energy to any interaction you have.

Do three incantations this morning before you leave the building. Then make a point of beaming at the first person you come into touch with. It may be your doorman, someone you pass on the way to work, your children, relatives, or someone else. Greet them in such a way that they smile and wonder, "What has gotten into them today!"

Speak with vigour. This means you'll talk louder, use different tones, maintain solid eye contact, gesticulate, and have fun. All you've worked on should come together in such a way that people are blown away just by interacting with you. It's also fine if they're feeling stressed. It is encouraged to go overboard.

You should not need to concentrate on every single moment of eye contact or gesticulation because you've done enough individual training. Rather, concentrate on the energy you have and the energy you give off. If you get down in the middle of the day, find a quiet place to do three more incantations and get back into a happy, hopeful frame of mind.

DAY 28: EXAMINE YOUR CHARISMATIC CONVICTIONS

Last chance to test charismatic belief. We'll repeat this exercise one more time before calling it a month.

Review your original charismatic conviction sheet and consider which third conviction will have the greatest effect if you increased the number of convictions to ten (pick a different one than you did on the first two times).

This is the one you'll be focusing on today. So, right now, rewrite all of the excuses you do have to believe it.

DAY 29 – HAVING A GOOD TIME AND PLAYING AROUND

Today is the second to last day. We're nearly there!

Today's goal will be created by integrating the skill sets that we've been working on.

We're going to annoy people. Play games like the rest of the country. For full impact, this will necessitate dedication, vocal range, and expansive comedic gesticulations.

The people you're with are the most important to mess around with. So, while you might consider ignoring the waiter, taxi driver, cashier, or elevator passenger next to you, these are the most important people because they are the ones that surround you. If you can develop the habit of being playful and jovial wherever you are, you will be able to carry the habit with you wherever you go.

So screw with the people who work with you, your mates, and your coworkers. Smiles and laughter are contagious.

DAY 30 – EVALUATION

It's time to take a breather and assess our current situation.

Eyes Do you make direct eye contact with others?

Do you have squinted eyes?

Do you have a grin on your face?

the voice

Are you making a lot of noise?

Is your voice low-pitched, or do you have an upward inflexion?

Are you solid at the end of your sentences, or do you falter?

Do you use character accents and a wide variety of voices while telling stories?

Have you figured out what your filler terms are and gotten rid of them?

Are you keeping an open body language?

Are you making a lot of gestures?

Do you have proper balance (in your shoulders)? (How are your hips?)

Such attitudes and actions

Are you able to capture people's attention with your stories?

Are you exuding positive energy (open body language, effusive speech, smiling eyes) everywhere you go?

Have you honed your responses to the questions "Where are you from?" and "What do you do?" to make them more engaging?

Are you willing to take "risks" in conversation? Are you cracking jokes? Speaking your mind, even though it's unpopular? Taking a firm stance on topics while others are unsure?

Are you tampering with people? With complete strangers? If you have any friends? What about your teammates and boss?

Do you think it will work out?

What areas have seen the most progress? What have you managed to keep up with this month? What activities did you engage in for a day or two and then abandon?

This 30-day workout can be repeated as many times as you want. Alternatively, concentrate on the workouts that were most beneficial to you.

Congratulations on completing the challenge!